That's Disgusting

That's Disgusting

An Adult Guide to What's Gross, Tasteless, Rude, Crude, and Lewd

GRETA GARBAGE

TEN SPEED PRESS
Berkeley, California

To my husband, who thinks disgusting things are appalling.

TEN SPEED PRESS
PO Box 7123
Berkeley, California 94707
www.tenspeed.com

Distributed in Australia by Simon and Schuster Australia, in Canada by Ten Speed Press Canada, in New Zealand by Southern Publishers Group, in South Africa by Real Books, and in Southeast Asia by Berkeley Books.

Cover Design by Lisa Patrizio
Interior Design by Jeff Brandenburg/ImageComp

Library of Congress Cataloging-in-Publication Data

Garbage, Greta, 1942–
    That's disgusting : an adult guide to what's gross, tasteless, rude, crude, and lewd / Greta Garbage.
        p.   cm.
    Includes bibliographical references (pp. 165–67) and index.
    ISBN 1-58008-094-4
    1. Human behavior Humor.   2. Body, Human Humor.   3. Hygiene Humor.
    I. Title.
    PN6231.H763G37   1999
    818'.5402—dc21   99-27896
                                                                              CIP

FIRST PRINTING, 1999
PRINTED IN CANADA

    4 5 6 7 8 9 10 — 05 04 03

Contents

Author's Introduction

What's in this book is disgusting, disturbing—and totally fascinating. Most other books leave out the dark and dirty parts; here, nothing is held back. Whether it's kinky sex or farting facts or toilet discussions or celebrity penises or perverse performances or shitting in space or freaks or sexual asphyxia or vaginal juices or fartleberries or smegma, you'll find it among the 1000-plus stories here.

Never before have tidbits been so titillating. Secrets so sick. History so horrific. News so nauseating. Crimes so crass. Facts so fulsome. And never before has one book included so much of this shocking stuff in one place. True, some of the stories are repelling—but most of them are so *com*pelling that you won't be able to stop reading.

It's good for you to read this, too, because the more grossness you're exposed to, the less gross everything will seem. And raising the limit on your "disgusting meter" can be good for you, your relationships, and maybe even society as a whole, because it makes you a more accepting and understanding person.

People think it's bad to keep pushing the envelope, but Pablo Picasso once said that the chief enemy of creativity is good taste.

An example of this was the advent of rock'n'roll and Elvis Presley. When they first appeared on the music scene, people were shocked (shocked!) and considered such music, with its open sensuality, totally disgusting. Some even demanded that it be banned.

But where would contemporary music be today if we hadn't accepted the once unacceptable? And how about Shakespeare, whose writing was once considered disgusting trash? Or statues like Michelangelo's *David*, which even recently was partially covered after being declared tasteless?

History contains hundreds of thousands of examples of cutting-edge culture—books, art, music, dance—that was once considered shocking and disgusting, not to be viewed, read, listened to, or danced to. Becoming more receptive and less condemning of the "disgusting," and being open to breaking taboos, can help us to accept these cultural innovations and advance as a society.

Immunizing yourself to the "disgusting" can also help you in your own relationships and your understanding of others. Oscar Wilde once stated, "Vulgarity is the behavior of others." People find certain acts repelling when *others* perform them, but not necessarily when *they* do.

As a simple example, all people pick their noses, yet are horrified to see others pick *their* noses. But since everyone has some disgusting (often hidden) habits, we as human beings should be more tolerant and accepting of all behavior that doesn't harm others, and should not judge others solely on the basis of what we think of some of their activities or habits.

Another reason it's good to increase your acceptance level is that it helps bridge age and culture gaps. A simple example here, too: Perhaps you think that piercing a tongue is absolutely vile—but after you read here about the piercing of *sexual* organs, piercing one's tongue or nose may seem almost benign.

Now, if it were your child who had pierced his or her tongue, and you had initially shunned him or her for doing it, your more liberal attitude could bring you closer. A lot of people, especially when they get older, close their minds to new and "disgusting" things. This creates a gap between these people and the ones who espouse and accept such things—usually the younger generation—and keeps the disapproving person a prisoner of old-fashioned ways of thinking, stuck in a certain "age warp."

Another reason it's good to increase your acceptance level is that it helps

This rigidity of disapproval is also found in our attitude toward societies other than ours, and toward times earlier than this one. Much that we find abhorrent today was perfectly acceptable at other times in history, and still is in countries other than ours.

A mild example: Some cultures have freely exposed the female breast in public, but thought that showing the *foot* was revolting.

Another example of the relativity of revulsion: bestiality. As a society, we abhor this practice, yet some societies in the past not only sanctioned women's fooling around sexually with monkeys, but even included bestiality in their religious rites.

THAT'S DISGUSTING

So sit back and don't fight the trip on the vomit comet. After you get a taste for the tasteless, buy *That's Disgusting Too: The 200 Most Disgusting Sites on the Internet* by this same author and use the Internet to find even more of what's outrageous, audacious, and hellacious.

Important: Neither the publisher nor the author is responsible for the cost of a new suit or dress if you throw up on your old one while reading this. Nor are we responsible for the cost of more analysis if something upsets you so much that you need extra sessions with your shrink. Or whatever else you can think of.

You also should *not* try anything you read in this book; it's presented for recreational and informational purposes only.

And finally, some of the material that follows *is* indeed disgusting. That's the reason for this book's title. That's why you bought it. *If you have a queasy stomach, or if you're underage, or if you can't deal with gross-outs, don't read this book.*

You have been warned.

Greta Garbage
GretaGarbage@aol.com
www.gretagarbage.com

Ass, Bizarre Objects Up and In

If you've ever wondered what your boss has up his ass, you may find out at an unorthodox site on the Internet* that describes **foreign objects found up the ass.** This weird alcove of medical knowledge contains commentary on, and confirmed cases of, **extremely bizarre objects** thrust into the fundaments of people generally seeking anal gratification.

These odd items people have stuck up their down staircase had to be delicately removed later—which is how they came to light, literally. Most of the victims would no doubt have preferred to have crawled off and hidden forever rather than have gone to a doctor or emergency room and explained how they got these things up their asses.

For example:

- Several **magazines,** such as *The Church Times,* have been retrieved from the anus. These were not found in the three people who had flashlights found in them, so apparently no one stuck the flashlights up there so they could read these magazines.

- **A microwave egg boiler,** inserted by a man attempting to relieve his intractable constipation.

- A **light bulb,** which the embarrassed unfortunate said he inserted while drunk. (It took suction-cup darts, mineral oil, and three catheters with inflated balloons in order to remove it.)

- A **shaving cream can,** which the person said he had inserted in order to collect on a bet of $100.

---

* For disgusting sites on the Internet see *That's Disgusting Too: The 200 Most Disgusting Sites on the Internet* also by Greta Garbage (me!).

Other weird items that came to light where the sun don't shine:

- A **frozen fish** (with the dorsal fin extended).
- A bottle of **Mrs. Butterworth's Syrup.**
- A pair of **reading glasses.**
- A **salami.**
- **Marijuana.**
- A **curling iron.**
- **Baseballs** (two of them).
- A frozen **pig's tail.**
- A **kangaroo tumor.**
- A **whip handle.**

Some of these objects were inserted to relieve constipation, or on a dare; but **most were placed there for sexual reasons.** Still, some of the victims came up with some pretty cheeky explanations of how these things got into their behinds. Generally, they tried to convince their doctors or emergency room personnel that they fell onto these objects—often after slipping in the shower.

Proof of the mendacity of these excuses came from the man who went to the doctor to help him remove a ketchup bottle that was up his tush. He claimed he had fallen on the bottle, but he couldn't explain how the bottle happened to have to have a condom slipped over the top.

Some men even had flashlights up their asses, facing up, but *without batteries.* This made nonsense of their claims that the flashlights had been inserted to look for something up there.

Hard-on: One of the most famous cases of rectal foreign bodies occurred when two men were fooling around, mixed some concrete, put it in a funnel, and one **poured the concrete into the other's rectum.**

After the concrete hardened, it stubbornly refused to be—well, eliminated. When it finally was removed by surgery, the boys ended up with a perfect concrete cast of the unfortunate victim's rectum, right up to grooves that were consistent with his rectal mucosal folds.

What concrete use he made of his unusual souvenir was not recorded in the medical literature.

Munitions dump: Military supplies such as shells have also been found in the rear. For example, one man **lost a bullet up his ass** when he used the shell to insert the suppository.

But the most bizarre case in this area concerned an old World War II veteran who had such bad hemorrhoids that they would get stuck in the seam of his underpants.

To get them out of the way, he often **pushed one particularly troublesome and protuberant hemorrhoid back up** with the artillery shell from an antiaircraft gun.

On one occasion, however, the shell got stuck, necessitating a visit to a surgical unit. The doctors were about to remove it when one of them casually asked, "It *is* spent, isn't it?"

"Oh, no!" said the man. "There's enough ammo in that shell to blast a Messerschmidt out of the sky."

They had to call in an army bomb squad—a "boob squad" would have been more appropriate for him—who then carefully built a lead box around his anus and defused the shell *in situ* before removing it.

In two recent ridiculous cases, ding-a-lings somehow got **telephones up their rectums.** In one case, in Munich, when a man collapsed, his phone somehow ended up in him, supposedly causing the redial button to become activated.

When his wife answered the call, she became worried because she heard inexplicable gurgling sounds. She called the police, who investigated, and were no doubt shocked to learn that this time they had a real asshole on the phone!

In another case, a "Darwin winner"—the Darwin Award is jocularly given to people who have removed themselves from the gene pool in a spectacular way—a Georgia attorney was showering with his cell phone.

He allegedly slipped on a tile, tripped against his dog, and **sat on his cell phone.** The cover somehow opened, activating the phone, or so he said.

Also in the hard-to-believe department, the phone supposedly rang three times during the lengthy surgical procedure undertaken to remove the phone. The doctors claimed that they were hysterical each time it happened. And perhaps also a bit disappointed that they hadn't found an answering machine up there as well.

Another anal insertion and Darwin winner, this one in Thailand, was reported by the *Japan Times*. It seems a horny thirteen-year-old was literally full of hot air after practicing a dangerous but popular masturbatory technique called pumping.

This technique gained some notoriety in America a few years ago when **Brigitte Nielsen** allegedly spread the rumor that **Sylvester Stallone had pumped his penis** because of difficulties he was said to be having getting an erection as a result of all the steroids he was rumored to have used. (And speaking of asses, how's this last sentence for covering the author's ass legally?)

In the Thai case, the boy was in the habit of **inserting a bicycle pump up his ass** so the air would give him a strong though ephemeral high. But this time, this jerk used compressed air at a gas station.

When he exploded, "one woman thought she was watching a twilight fireworks display and started clapping," according to the newspaper report reprinted in "This Is True."

Another comment, almost as foolish, came from a hospital spokesman: "This act is a sin against God. Inflate your tires by all means, but then hide your bicycle pump where it cannot tempt you."

One thing no one wants **up their ass is a prison guard's finger.** So eight prisoners in Montana decided not just to complain about rectal searches, but to be paid back for the humiliation.

They sued the state for the degradation inflicted upon them, but the jury was unmoved. They sent the message "Up yours" by awarding only $9 to each prisoner. (This seems especially unfair because the act would usually cost at least $100 on the street.)

Finally, no one wants anal fistulas up their ass—they can make sitting down extremely uncomfortable. According to a book called *Gross: A Compendium of the Unspeakable, Unpalatable, Unjust, and Appalling*, the British national anthem, "God Save the King," was originally written as a French song to celebrate King Louis XIV's successful recovery from anal fistulas.

In the U.S. the song is known as "My Country, 'Tis Of Thee," so the next time you hear that song and stand up, think of those before you who have had to stand up for different reasons.

ON THE LIGHTER SIDE

A man goes to a proctologist for **unexplained anal pain.** The doctor finds a rose up the man's ass.

"How on Earth did that get there?" asks the patient incredulously.

"I'll go back and see if there's a card," says the doc.

Bathroom Privacy

Everyone cherishes his or her privacy on the john, whether at home or away. So you can imagine the horror of a passenger on an Air France jet who was minding his own business while doing his business when French crew members broke open the door and **pulled him off the toilet with his pants down.** They dragged him into the passenger section of the plane, leaving him embarrassingly exposed.

It turned out the smoke alarm had malfunctioned, signaling that he had lit up a cigarette when he hadn't. He later sued for $12 million. (If he thinks the French were rude to him on the plane, he should try a French restaurant.)

King Louis XIV, the Sun King would **relieve himself in front of others,** on the other kind of throne.

He was also quite partial to enemas—in the final year of his life he averaged more than one a day—and would hold court for hours for the lucky few on **enema days.**

Perhaps he should have been called the Moon King.

The most famous contemporary person to **defecate without regard to privacy** was **former president Lyndon Johnson.** An earthy man, he once said that he wanted someone to "kiss my ass in Macy's window and say it smells like roses," and that he didn't trust a man "unless I've got his pecker in my pocket."

Biographers wrote that Johnson liked to go to the bathroom in the middle of a discussion—and would insist that the person he was talking to join him in the john while he was literally shooting the shit.

Before he became President, if he was in a hotel where it was cooler in the hall bathroom if the door was left open, he left it open, even if he was on the toilet.

This confirmed for the voters that he was full of shit, even before the rest of the country decided that on the basis of his policies with respect to the Vietnam War.

The philosopher **Diogenes** may have been looking for an honest man, but he wasn't looking for a place to crap in private. He would evacuate right in the marketplace, believing it ridiculous to demand privacy for such matters.

ON THE LIGHTER SIDE

It's been said that the only time the world beats a path to your door is when you're in the bathroom.

Bizarre Sex and the Wild Kink-dom

Bestiality has been considered the one taboo too taboo to break. However, this hasn't always been the case. The ruling deity in the Greek Pantheon was Zeus, who was fond of taking the form of an animal in order to seduce his *femme du jour*. Numerous works of art show Leda being ravished by Zeus in the form of a swan, and one wonders whether the artists were entirely motivated by the Muse.

Some aren't interested in engaging in bestiality as much as in *watching* this unnatural human behavior. Indeed, bestiality was a form of entertainment in the same Roman arena that offered nude Olympics and gladiators battling starved lions, who would chew up a few gaunt saints.

But these "gladiators" got really gross. They were brought into the arena with **animals trained to copulate with people**—either vaginally or anally. No wonder the Roman Empire fell!

"Eskimo kisses" are just the tip of the iceberg. Copper Eskimos, from the Arctic coast of North America, engaged in **intercourse not only with live animals, but with dead ones as well.** A result, no doubt, of all those cold lonely nights with no two-legged friends to trade a bit of the hard for a bit of the soft.

Some in the Middle East believe that, "after having sexual relations with a lamb, it is a mortal sin to eat its flesh." Does that mean it's OK for Mary (or Muhammad) to have a little lamb if **Mary (or Muhammad) screws the little lamb** but doesn't eat it afterwards? (It's one thing to screw up your cooking, but quite another to cook up your screwing.)

Some sweat the petty things and some pet the sweaty things. In Lebanon, a man is supposedly legally entitled to **have sex with an animal—but only if it's female.** If it's male, the crime is punishable by death.

What exactly was she trying to say? A very close friend of **Jerzy Kosinski,** author of *Being There*, *The Painted Bird*, and so on, wrote an article about this notoriously kinky genius in *New York* magazine.

After noting what a complicated man he was, she wrote, **"Having sex with barnyard animals is fine** if you've written *The Painted Bird*. I'm not attracted to oxen."

A few years ago, a New Zealand judge sentenced a sixteen-year-old boy to seven years in prison for "congress with a sheep." Then he suspended the sentence, explaining, **"Society no longer frowns on sex with sheep."**

Which society does this judge belong to? (Maybe this type of folly in the fields explains why New Zealand is not a world power.)

Some people would be sheepish about buying one, but some sex shops sell an inflatable sheep doll called **"Love Ewe."** The sheep has an opening under its tail.

ON THE LIGHTER SIDE

"What do you call a desert dweller walking with **a pig and a sheep?**"
Bisexual.

Bizarre Sex with Dogs

As long as dogs have been domesticated, people have been giving the dog a bone, or, as they say, **putting the noodle to the poodle;** aka smooch the pooch, derrière the terrier, or cock the spaniel.

However, not many people admit to loving their dogs *quite* that much. Some people will admit that part of the reason they walk their dogs a lot is that a cute dog, unlike a cute human, can usually get a conversation started, possibly with a potential mate.

Perhaps, though, that guy in a suit walking his golden retriever, or that woman with the big German shepherd, has already found one.

Bestiality with dogs isn't even considered that serious a crime in some places. For example, in Thailand, **if a man rapes a dog, he is charged—** with cruelty to animals.

Some pervert was having sex with his dog when he changed his mind—definitely a problem, since a "knot" near the base of a dog's frankfurter expands during an erection, guaranteeing that if you buy the ticket, you'll take the ride.

But this dog's penis remained stuck in his rectum, leaving him with a literal pain in the ass. Indeed, he ultimately needed medical help to handle the penalty for early withdrawal.

People have been injured allowing their dogs to lick their sexual organs. Doctors report that women have developed hard-to-treat vaginal infections—especially since they don't tell their doctors how they got these, making them harder for the docs to diagnose or cure.

Both sexes have also been injured by overamorous or overanxious dogs. For example, one patient who rubbed his genitalia with raw hamburger, to encourage his dog got to come and get it, got chewed up when his dog got more excited about getting it than about coming.

I've got a lover-ly bunch of coconuts: Getting a dog to eat, or getting its owner excited, by placing food in the genital area is perfectly acceptable in some tribes. Trukese women of the Pacific liked to place **coconut meat in their vaginas** and then have a dog eat it out.

Both men and women of the Kurtachis, also in the Pacific, don't treat their mates like dogs, but treat their dogs like mates. According to *The Sex Chronicles*, if they are unable to pair up with each other, they consider it perfectly acceptable to **have sex with whatever nice single dogs are around.**

69 the K9! A veterinarian claims that **a dog's penis is three times cleaner than a man's penis.** Probably true, since a dog spends considerable time each day cleaning his "lipstick" with his tongue.

Now, some women look at that and think, "Well, what do you expect from a guy?" And some men look at it and say, "Wow, I wish I could do that all day, especially when I've got nothing to do because my computer broke down. "

But according to *277 Secrets Your Dog Wants You to Know*, **excessive ball licking by your dog** could be a sign of problems such as allergies, fleas, skin problems, or even brucellosis, which is a venereal disease in dogs. (Dogs can get two different kinds of venereal disease.)

So if your dog suddenly starts licking his balls a lot, speak to a vet. But if he's been doing it for years, leave him alone, because you've got one happy dog there.

Ballsy maneuvers: Neuticles are **plastic testicles,** implanted into neutered dogs, which are said to have the look and feel of a "Gummi Bear."

Why should dogs wear such silly things? The inventor says it's so the castrated dog won't feel different from other dogs, which he might if he looked around and noticed he was missing something.

The inventor once lobbied Bill Clinton to have him implant neuticals in the First Dog, Buddy, after his castration operation. Perhaps if *Clinton* had been the one given plastic balls, he could have kept himself out of the doghouse.

ON THE LIGHTER SIDE

In February of 1999, at the famous Westminster dog show, one of the dogs **relieved himself of his diarrhea** right in the middle of the ring at a critical moment in the show.

Sportscaster Bill Weir, after reporting on this said, "You almost never see this type of thing in the Miss America competition."

Bizarre Sex with Horses

L ittle things mean a lot, but this is taking it one step too far. Humans, perhaps the world's most sexually indiscriminate animals, have managed to get sexual pleasure from snakes, octopi, eels, fish, birds, fruit, trees, even insects. But next to dogs, they have most often ridden—alas, not always in the traditional sense—horses.

Some have also used horses for sex in another way. Lots of husbands have seen their wives entranced by TV shows and movies about horses, and some have even bought their wives horses. Did they know that many women achieve orgasm while riding a horse—which is perhaps more than they get from riding their husbands? (In any case, it's certainly more romantic than a spin cycle.)

It has been whispered about more than one historical figure that they were "in a stable relationship" with the horses they rode on (or vice versa). **Catherine the Great** is the most famous for this.

But actually, despite the rumors that she died under the saddle, she died from a plain old cerebral hemorrhage, on her way to the toilet, when she was sixty-five years old. She had been making it with a twenty-seven-year-old, who perhaps was *hung* like a horse, which could be how the legend got started.

Mark Matthews, the author of *The Horseman*, **so loved his mare that he not only "kept her" but married her.** It was an actual wedding, and he even made pink "hooflets" and lingerie for the ceremony. Indeed, he was so eager to be a good groom to his horse that he even had a penile implant so he could satisfy her better. But after all this, it's been reported that he's unfaithful, since he keeps another horse. (But for what?)

A walk on the wild side: Jerry Springer, in one episode of his infamous talk show that was titled **"I Married a Horse,"** featured the man above revealing the revolting details of his five-year sexual relationship with his horse.

But even Jerry Springer can go too far. Also on the show was **a woman who had a love affair with her dog.** A number of TV stations refused to air the show. Why can't we all just get along?

The ancient Hittites, in 1400 B.C., created some interesting legal loopholes to permit fornication with their favorite fun animals. If a man "did evil" with cattle, he could be executed. But he'd receive no punishment if he, er, **got in the saddle with his stallions.**

ON THE LIGHTER SIDE

You thought the Mad Hatter threw a wild tea party? According to actor Patrick Swayze's caterer, Swayze threw a tea party for his Arabian horses. No one knows **what kind of horsing around** went on during the party.

Bizarre Sex with Unusual Animals

Yes, there are weirdos who make it with dogs and horses and other animals but they *don't* make it with gerbils. And no, Richard Gere didn't. He fell prey to rumors about this nonexistent perversion, which is allegedly performed with a cardboard tube, providing a small gerbil easy tunneling access to the ass. Once it gets there, the promised pleasure comes from the animal's twitching around as it burrows in and makes itself at home.

Despite all the people who say they know someone who was at a hospital when someone was brought in with a furry ferret up their fundament, there is no known case of anyone's actually putting a gerbil up their rectum, according to a debunking newsgroup on the Internet called alt.folk-lore.urban.

On the other hand, gerbils may have been used for another purpose in ancient China. The Chinese were said to have used these rodents for torture—and ultimately death—by inserting the animal and then closing off the rear exit, letting the gerbil unsuccessfully try to chew its way out of the body. (The only problem is that an hour after eating a Chinese, the rodent is hungry again.)

Cleopatra may have found an unusual animal for sex, allegedly developing an early-edition "vibrator" with a box of **live bees**, which she supposedly put on her honeypot for a sweet experience.

As outrageously untrue as this story sounds, there are reports of some **men who encourage bees to sting their penises** to make them swell and become more sensitive. This supposedly brings them pleasure, unless they're the one person in twenty who is allergic to bee venom, who could die from this stinging activity. (To bee or not to bee, that is the question for them.)

Here are a few other animal tales reprinted in the (sick) sexual literature:

- Besides bees, some **women have smeared honey on their vulvas to get flies** to fly to them and stimulate them. (This is how "old wives" found that honey draws more flies than vinegar.)

- Roman women were reported to have used the **heads of live snakes** and the **tails of live fish for vaginal insertion**, masturbating as the creatures tried to crawl out.

- Indeed, in a recent case, a woman developed a vaginal infection after using **live eels to induce an orgasm**. (An electric eel could have given her an even bigger charge.)

- Snakes alive! There are also ancient as well as current reports of **women inserting nondangerous snakes** for a slithery experience.

Monkeying around: Some Amazon women were so tough that they **rejected the company of men for monkeys.** Monkeys were also part of a religious ritual practiced by the Hindus. They accepted bestiality with sacred animals, going ape over a monkey god. They worshiped him, keeping white-bearded apes (known as Lord Baboons) in temples, where **the monkeys served as part-time sexual playthings** for pious women.

Herodotus mentions religious women in Egypt who **got it on with goats.** (Maybe because they were nannies.)

Don't have a cow, man: A fifty-year-old Swede paid a visit to some cows and filmed his sick activities. He then brought the film to a local photo company to get it developed. (Bessie, is that *you?*)

The only thing that developed for him was a jail sentence, proving that if someone's going to have **a roll in the hay with the farm animals,** it helps to be smarter than one.

After a while, crocodile: Most people think the only thing to do with a crocodile—other than avoid one—is to turn the wretchedly ugly creature into a pocketbook. But some perverts have a different idea.

When the female crocodile is copulating, she lies on her back; she has a great deal of trouble righting herself afterward. There are reports in the literature of Egyptian men who have taken sexual advantage of these supine, helpless beasts. (Not to be confused with Hollywood actresses being taken advantage of these days by lounge lizards.)

Deer me: Even in bestiality circles, the following behavior just ruins it for all normal deer fornicators. According to *Strange Days #2*, the police in Bethel Park, Pennsylvania, found a five-day-old headless deer carcass in the apartment of a thirty-two-year old local man.

He admitted that he had found his deer-ly beloved, taken it home, **fornicated with it, drunk its blood,** and kept it around in case he could think of anything else to do with it. (Ever hear of venison?)

Just horny: Speaking of deers and sex, did you ever see a deer rub its antlers against a tree, or lower its head to rub the ground? **What the deer is actually doing is masturbating.** If you don't believe it, focus your attention away from the head, and you'll see that the deer's dong becomes erect as he rubs. Actually, the antlers and the penis are so connected in a deer, that the antlers grow as his penis does.

ON THE LIGHTER SIDE

In 1750, **a man was sentenced to death for intercourse with a she— ass.** (Some men think the term redundant.) Historically, the animals involved were also often burned with their "lovers," since they were generally considered to be as responsible for the act as the people involved. But in this famous case, the ass was acquitted and freed, because it was said that the donkey had not freely participated in the lewd act.

Blow Jobs, Dangers of

Oral sex is occasionally fatal; for example, if the man literally performs a blow job, that is, actually **blows air into a woman's vagina,** he risks killing her with an air embolism. Or, if the man jams his love sausage into the woman's mouth too hard, the woman can die from **impaction of the penis in the pharynx.** And men can almost wish they were dead if the partner has **epilepsy** and has a muscle spasm of the jaw during oral sex.

A bizarre blow job death occurred recently in Australia when a thirty-four-year-old man drowned a twenty-five-year-old **woman who was fellating him underwater.** He held her under too long, continuing to hold her head underwater until he came. He claimed later that he had confused her death throes with sexual ecstasy.

The most highly publicized case of blow job death was in Italy in the 1950s, when a **seventeen-year-old woman choked to death on semen** during an orgy attended by high-level government officials. (Most of them became low-level government officials afterward.)

In the '70s, a man in Germany was sentenced for **killing a newborn child by utilizing her sucking reflex** to get him off. The baby, too, choked to death when her throat filled up with semen.

As disgusting as this is, there are several similar cases in the literature of **adults using newborns for sex,** although it rarely leads to death. Even the famed Roman Caesar Tiberius was said to have used unweaned babies to suck him off.

It isn't only men who use babies for blow jobs. **One of Charles Manson's followers, Susan Atkins, boasted that she had started fellating her infant son** soon after he was born.

ON THE LIGHTER SIDE

Almost as sick as **Susan Atkins's phallic osculation** was the name she gave her son: Zezozose Zadfrack Glutz.

Body Boogers and Disgusting Parts

As lovely as humans can look after a solid hour or so of grooming, anyone who's ever looked in the mirror in the morning knows that the longer you let it go, the more you look like a Skid Row bum.

Physicists dismiss things like this as "entropy" but most people just rub out the eye-boogers, cough up the phlegm, wipe off the dingleberries, splash water on their faces, and get to work twenty minutes late.

Actually, many physicists never bother picking out their eye-boogers or removing dingleberries, and hence manage to have time to come up with words like *entropy.*

Ears one for the books: Some people **eat the waxy buildup out of their ears.** Worse still, one woman was spotted in Spain **munching casually on her eye-boogers** (also known as eye crust, which contains urea, as in you-know-what). Don't cry for me, señorita!

That crud in the baby's bed is not necessarily dandruff. It's called **cradle crap,** and it's caused by leftover chemicals from the mother's body. They make oil glands in the baby's head become active after birth.

Ever wonder what causes a **belly button booger** as you stare at it, pick it, or eat it? It's lint, mainly from your clothing, which sticks to the sweat and remains there after the moisture departs.

Bezoars are repulsive bundles of hair, vegetable fibers, or food that form in the stomachs of humans (and animals). Incredibly, **Queen Elizabeth I** had a bezoar included in her crown jewels.

Sometimes bezoars become large enough to cause trouble. One woman **chewed her hair** enough for a bezoar to form; it was large enough that it had to be surgically removed.

Put that in your crown, Queen Elizabeth!

Chew on this one for a while: If a tooth gets really rotten, a pus-filled hole, or abscess, can form underneath it. Sometimes germs from this abscess attack the gums and form a **gumboil.** If this bursts, the mouth fills with vile-tasting pus.

Shut yo' mouth cause if you gotta go, urine for a mouthful: When a person pees, a small deposit of **urine enters the mouth** via the saliva glands. (This distinguishes the normal person from the politician, who talks shit instead.)

Toe jam (or Chee-toes) comes from bacteria dining on the fatty acids in the sweat that pours out of the foot's pores. But it's not only dead bacteria that give that gunk between your toes a bad odor; it's also their piles of waste. So **shouldn't toe jam be called toe turds?**

ON THE LIGHTER SIDE

Over three-fourths of household dust is made of **dead skin cells.** Since it's said that we change our cells entirely every seven years, if you didn't empty your vacuum cleaner for that long, that would be *you* in there!

Body Parts of Famous People

The brain is a gelatinous colloidal mass that has been responsible for all of civilization, from the heights of art and literature, the *Mona Lisa* and the works of Shakespeare, to the depths of human depravity, such as, well, this book.

One brain that's caused a great deal of interest is the one that belonged to President John F. Kennedy—mainly because it disappeared. (President Reagan topped this by having his brain disappear while he was *alive* and still in office.)

Other than its obvious souvenir value, why would any official type want JFK's brain? Because Kennedy's brain might prove that there *was* a conspiracy to kill him and his death was not the work of a lone loon.

If the wound in Kennedy's neck was an entry wound, he was shot from the front—in other words, from the Grassy Knoll. If it was an exit wound, as was claimed, the shot could have come from behind—that is, from Lee Harvey Oswald's gun at the Texas Schoolbook Depository window.

But we'll never know, because **no one knows what happened to John Kennedy's brain.**

Was Einstein also a no-brainer? **Albert Einstein's brain** was kept "for future study." According to *Strange Days #1*, parts of the brain were stolen at his autopsy and then "stored in three jars under the sink in a tiny apartment of a doctor."

That doctor gave pieces of the brain to another doctor as a Christmas present. He distributed some to still another friend, while the first doctor kept Einstein's brain in his refrigerator and labeled it "Big Al's Brain." Several fragments are now privately owned by Einstein's admirers.

Marilyn Monroe's famous breasts were somehow destroyed (stolen?) during her autopsy, and a makeup artist had to create artificial breasts for her when preparing her for burial. Presumably her other parts were intact, including her six toes on one foot (maybe the extra one was for fetishists to fantasize sucking on).

And here's an even weirder "body part" of hers that someone claims they have. An artist has a sealed vial that, he says, contains **a fart from Marilyn Monroe,** for which he supposedly paid a lot of money.

Rub me tender: Years ago, someone who wanted him, needed him, and loved him made an unsuccessful attempt to steal Elvis's body. That failed, but **Elvis Presley** would probably be all shook up to know that one of his most ardent fans loved him so tenderly that this Georgia woman somehow managed to obtain for her collection of Elvis mementos—**one of Elvis's warts.**

Big Al's eyes: In addition to the brain fragments that are floating around, **Albert Einstein's eyeballs were later found in a jar** and, even more humiliating, in New Jersey. (Everything's relative.)

One of his doctors spent twenty minutes disconnecting the eyes after Einstein's death so he could keep them as a little memento. They were auctioned off in 1994. In addition, Big Al's heart and intestines may also have been removed and kept by others.

Franz Josef Haydn may have been best known during his life for his "Surprise Symphony," but the biggest surprise for him came after his death. **His head was stolen** by a phrenologist searching for the "faculty of music."

That man then gave it to a woman who displayed it in a glass case for eleven years at her musical soirées. It wasn't until 1954, almost 150 years after Haydn died, that his head and body were finally reunited.

In the 1800s, **Burke and Hare** were responsible for at least sixteen murders, committed to obtain body parts for surgeons to dissect and study. But one of them became a victim of the body parts mania himself.

Some of the skin from William Burke's body was circulated to ghoulish collectors after he was hanged in 1829 for his crimes. Who ended up with some of it? **Charles Dickens had a piece of Burke's skin,** which he used as a bookmark.

Novelist **Sir Walter Scott** somehow obtained a **stolen cervical vertebra of King Charles I.** He used it as a salt cellar, no doubt shaking up some of his famous guests, such as Queen Victoria. (No insult was intended; Scott just thought King Charlie was the salt of the earth.)

ON THE LIGHTER SIDE

A New York artist made a ring from one of **the gallstones of Larry Hagman** of *Dallas* fame. What gall!

(See also "Penises, Famous People's.")

Breasts

Titties, gazongas, mammalian protuberances, jugs, gourds, mammaries, globes, hooters—these jiggly attention-getters have dazzled blushing men (and, for that matter, women) since before decency, or something masquerading as decency, clothed them.

Yet modern society has been ambivalent—on the one hand hiding them, on the other, parading them. Terrified Victorians erected monstrous structures of steel and cloth to conceal them, yet also thrust them up and made the cleavage itself a stutter-inducing vista.

Society has also created implants so women can live up to the ideal, but a Maryland man was so upset over his breakup with his girlfriend that he stabbed her in the chest and **attempted to remove the breast implants** he had bought for her because he didn't want his successors to benefit from them.

After he was arrested for assault, the couple appeared together in court—breast friends once again you could say—and stated that despite what had happened, they wanted to stay together. After all, it was just a little tit for tat.

In another eerie case concerning transplants, a Columbia, South Carolina, woman couldn't get her insurance company to pay for the removal of her silicone breast implants, which had caused her a number of continuing health problems. So she simply took a razor and **cut out her own breast implants.**

The women of Africa's Nandi tribe thought they were making their breasts more beautiful by wearing two plate-shaped disks around their necks; these pressed against their breasts while they were developing. This eventually **elongated their tits,** leaving them hanging like strips of skin on an emaciated ninety-year-old woman.

They were so flat that mothers threw these jugs over their shoulders and nursed their babies on their backs. (Talk about "Baby's got back!")

These women apparently didn't mind their breasts ending up flat as a pancakes, since their men seemed to like them that way and were glad to provide the syrup.

(No) thanks for the mammaries: Many men develop female-type globes—one poor man had eight breasts—but one guy had an even harder time of it.

He had a **breast that grew on his right inner thigh.** And he couldn't lie and tell the curious that it was a wart or a tumor, because it was the size of a goose egg, was soft, and had an areola.

ON THE LIGHTER SIDE

A mail-order company received a large number of orders for a book called *Great Tits of Britain.* Disappointed purchasers received a book on the titmouse—which is called a tit for short.

Breath, Bad; Mouth and Teeth

Holy Halitosis! According to the *Journal of the Canadian Dental Association*, half the population has chronic bad breath, and a study found that most participants with garbage breath were **ignorant of their own mouth-stink**. Obviously their best friends didn't tell them.

If you're worried about having breath that could knock the Statue of Liberty off her perch, there are a few disgusting experiments you can perform. One study found that if you scrape the gunk off the back of your tongue with a spoon and take a whiff, you'll know how bad you really are.

Another study said to smell a finger moistened with your own saliva to determine whether you have bad breath. (You might want to stick that finger all the way down your throat and puke if it's really bad.)

Someone can **determine from your breath whether you have to fart.** According to *Tailwinds*, a researcher developed a test for excess hydrogen in a patient's breath; if it's present, you have gas in your intestines.

If you're not a hemorrhoid, get off my ass: Many people mistakenly **brush their teeth with Preparation H,** since the packaging of the famous hemorrhoid ointment is similar to that of a popular toothpaste.

By the way, here's a new wrinkle. Some women deliberately use Preparation H north of its intended target. They use it on their wrinkles—facial wrinkles, that is. And it's not just women who use it. Late night talk-show host **Conan O'Brien** admits that his makeup woman put it on his face—and it worked to get rid of his eyebags!

ON THE LIGHTER SIDE

"Frankly, my dear, I do give a damn," is what **Clark Gable**'s leading ladies probably were thinking when he kissed them during his movies. They may have initially been excited about getting a chance to play opposite America's greatest love symbol—until they got a sniff of the stud.

He wore dentures and was said to have extremely **bad breath**—so bad, in fact, that Vivian Leigh claimed later that she had to hold her breath during their famous kissing scenes.

Castration or Bobbitization

(Men: You may want to cross your legs before you read this section.)

Most men are horrified at the idea of having any pain inflicted on their tenderest parts, and feel a sympathetic twinge there at the mere suggestion of tampering. Or at a whisper of the name of Lorena Bobbitt, who proved that the penis is not mightier than the sword.

But while her case may have gotten the most publicity in recent times, it was not the worst. Indeed, **a sickening sexual story concerns the teenage cousin of Bill Clinton,** who, in 1985, when Bill was governor-elect, accused an Arkansas car mechanic of **raping her.**

Shortly thereafter, the children of the mechanic came home to find their father, the alleged rapist, on a chair, hog-tied; two thirds of his blood had leaked out of him, and his genitals were on the floor.

They were retrieved, and the county sheriff, a political ally of Clinton's, **displayed the testicles in a fruit jar** on his desk for quite a while. This moral slug proudly showed them off to visitors, but eventually flushed them down the toilet.

(By the way, the list of people involved with Clinton who have died, which has been circulated widely on the Internet, includes this sheriff, who died in 1998.)

Thai one off: In many cases in Thailand, men who couldn't keep their pricks in their pants later found them on the chopping block. (What do you expect in **a country so penis-obsessed** that a song titled "I'm Vasectomized" once hit #3 on the music charts?)

In one instance, after Bobbitizing her wayward lover, one jealous Thai woman threw his detached member out the window. The horrified new eunuch ran to the window to see where it was so he could retrieve it, only to watch a **duck waddling off with the man's dick dangling from its mouth.**

⊛

Ball loon: Another vengeful Thai castrator **tied the severed staff to a balloon and released it into the air.** Up, up, and away.

⊛

The unkindest cut. Have castrating women ever been proven wrong in their accusations about the men after cutting their jewels off? In the case of **Clinton's raped cousin,** mentioned above, the castrated rapist, who has been in jail for over fourteen years—the average time served for a rapist is only five and a half years—may be innocent. The young victim originally described another man as her rapist.

⊛

In a clear-cut case of innocence discovered too late, a Brazilian woman who found her husband in bed with their naked two-year-old daughter cut first and asked questions later.

She went off half-cocked (or at least her husband did) and **flushed her husband's jewels down the toilet.** Later, she found out that her child had climbed into bed with her innocent father after he had fallen asleep.

⊛

Stuck on him: At least it's a little more reversible when revenge-seeking women use **Krazy Glue** on a prick instead of a knife. Or Krazy Glue is *usually* reversible.

However, in one case, a cuckolded husband supposedly **cemented his wife's hands to her lover's love pump.** Despite surgery to separate the two, the lover supposedly died from the glue he absorbed.

Some reasons for castration:

⊛ Historically, people have been forcibly castrated to **prevent them from having more children.** *Simons' Book of World Sexual Records* (an incredible book on sexual history) reports that in 1790, in England, a mentally retarded man who had already fathered three children he couldn't handle was forcibly **castrated—without anesthetic—by the local pig butcher.**

- **Mementos after death:** In the 1700s, a Belgian woman removed her husband's favorite organs from his corpse, **ground the penis to a powder,** and used it as a remedy for her female complaints. .

- The all-time record of useless war mementos or **phallus capturing is over 13,000 pairs of testicles**—many of which were taken from the enemy soldiers while they were still alive.

- **Voice improvement,** or The Boys in the Band-Aid: As little as 100 years ago, Vatican choir boys were still being castrated so that they could retain their high singing voices. O Solo Me-ouch!

ON THE LIGHTER SIDE

There's a company that sells fake **"pickled pussy"** and **"penis fly trap"** plants, along with a joking see-through bottle of **"Tantalizing Testicles."** The slogan for this product is **"Pick a peck of pickled Peters."**

(Men: This section is finished and you can uncross your legs now.)

Castration, Voluntary

When the Heaven's Gate **wackos cut off their whackers,** it shocked the world, which rejected the belief that castrating oneself would bring one closer to God. (Still, many secretly agreed with the reasoning behind their actions, namely that sex is a distraction from spiritual matters.)

Nowadays, religious self-castration is considered tantamount to utter insanity, but castration as a religious ritual has a long history, too disgusting and boring—or frightening—to summarize. Typical example: the Russian Skoptsi, or so-called "Castrators," considered those members who cut off their entire penises to be more holy than those who "merely" cut off their testicles.

No hard feelings: While castrating oneself before a wedding would defeat the main purpose of most marriages, that hasn't stopped some groups from insisting on some form of symbolic removal. For example, in some Arab tribes, **the bride had to remove her groom's foreskin, along with the skin on the shaft of his penis.**

Even worse, she had to do it on the day of the wedding! The groom was then expected to perform sexually as if nothing had happened earlier. Talk about living (un)happily ever after!

Some primitive Arab tribes also made the groom-to-be **strip the skin off the entire length of his penis** in front of his future father-in-law.

Not surprisingly, many died. And if those who lived cried, they were then killed by their intended fathers-in-law, who considered them cowards and not manly enough for their daughters.

Usually, self-castration is the work of the disturbed, such as the Australian lunatic who not only cut off his genitals, but then **put them in a blender,** and later poured the liquefied contents into a box.

A refuge of the disturbed in America is the Jerry Springer show. One **man who castrated himself,** which was bad enough, then **appeared on the Jerry Springer show** to discuss it, which was almost worse.

"I used a tourniquet so I wouldn't bleed to death . . . used ice, used the pruning shears . . . and also used a pair of scissors," he said.

"I didn't remember flushing it," he added. "But it was the only thing I could have done and I drove myself to the hospital after. . . . It was a couple of days before I realized I had done it."

You think he'd have noticed it the first time he went to pee.

ON THE LIGHTER SIDE

A possible title for this segment on the Springer show, or any discussion of self-castration, would be "Take my balls—please!"

Cats and Sex

Anyone who's ever had a cat knows they're a little weird—even if they are wonderful. When you want to pet them, they're nowhere to be found, but if you want to read the newspaper they're instantly there, shredding it.

On top of that, they'll suddenly stare at nothing for no reason. Or do something with seemingly no rhyme. There are unverifiable anecdotes of cats raping chickens, for example, even though most people feel that chickens are sexless.

Here's some information about cat sexuality, mostly from *277 Secrets Your Cat Wants You to Know*, a fascinating book full of offbeat information about cats:

- **Some cats masturbate.**
- **Cats can have orgasms.**
- **A female cat has a tiny clitoris,** with a small bone in it.
- **Some cats like kinky things;** for example, some are turned on by being lightly spanked.
- By giving cats enemas and then playing different musical tones, it was established that **cats will have an orgasm when they hear a certain tone.** Even stranger, the same note will make kittens defecate. (It's E in the fourth octave, if you must know.)
- **Cats will have sex with a family member** (theirs and, at certain times of the month, yours, if they can).

Sexually satisfying a cat: People know that a female cat in heat is insatiable—and very noisy. Some have tried to shut up a furry friend by satisfying her with one of their own digits. But at least one person learned that the pen can be mightier than, say, the toe.

An adventurous beauty parlor operator found himself awake late one night as his in-heat feline cried and writhed for that special touch. When the cat assumed *the* position, he inserted a ballpoint pen with a tiny retractable nib in her vulva, and then kept clicking the top of the pen in and out until she came and quieted down.

Although it's not recommended for others, for him it was the write stuff.

ON THE LIGHTER SIDE

The **cat's penis is only three-fourths of an inch long**—but they sometimes lie and tell their feline partners it's an inch.

Circumcision, etc.

Circumcision is the most common surgical procedure in the U.S. But many who involuntarily had it as children now want their foreskins back, and are having surgery to get them. (Where are the foreskins coming from?)

In the meantime, hospitals are making money from foreskins, since the going rate is about **$35 per skin.** The skins have been sold to be used for producing fake skin for plastic surgery or interferon for cancer research.

Good news: Foreskin fanatics will be glad to note that interferon is now being made mostly from a bacillus.

Bad news: The bacillus grows on human feces.

Penis power, or souvenirs of war: During Biblical days, circumcision was considered proof of victory in battle. In the Bible (Samuel I), David was told by the king that he wanted a hundred foreskins of the Philistines instead of a dowry. David, a show-off, then killed 200 and brought the king their foreskins. The Bible says he then became the king's son-in-law—but it doesn't say what happened to the foreskins.

The Malaysian minister of culture once suggested that Malaysia have **mass circumcision ceremonies** to attract tourists. (They may be hoping to attract the kind who leave big tips.)

King Louis XVI had such an **abnormally overgrown foreskin** that his erections were painful and he couldn't enjoy sex.

It wasn't until he had been married for seven years that he had his foreskin removed. He lost his virginity on his twenty-third birthday, thanks in no small part to his adult circumcision.

Sew what??? Infibulation has been performed on men and women to cure masturbation and/or ensure chastity. When it's done to women, the

clitoris and the inner and outer lips of the vagina are removed and what's left is fastened shut. This leaves only a tiny opening to enable women to urinate and menstruate. Women have to be cut open later to make love and have children.

Sew bad! Infibulation is also practiced on men—by closing the penis off in some way. For example, **the foreskin is pulled down over the prick,** holes are made in it, and it is sewed together. Or the scrotum may be sewed around the staff. Either method, needless to say, affects erection—and, in some cases, sanity.

ON THE LIGHTER SIDE

Do people who were circumcised and now want their foreskins back suffer from **foreskin envy**?

Cleanliness and Bacteria

No shit: Excrement contains a lot of **disgusting bacteria**—many of them still alive—and over 120 viruses, including hepatitis A. If the bacteria would just stay in the toilet, the world would be a lot different. But because most people's personal hygiene habits are so poor, *E. coli* has been found everywhere.

Germ warfare: According to Dr. Charles Gerba, a microbiologist in Arizona who calls himself "the **Sultan of Slime,**" **the bathroom is cleaner then the kitchen** in the average house. Not that you'll want to mix a salad in the toilet bowl. But he says you're safer making a sandwich on top of the toilet bowl than in the kitchen.

That sinking feeling: Gerba says that besides the sink, the **dirtiest spots** in the kitchen (where you may find things that belong in the bathroom!) are dishcloths, cutting boards, sponges, and sink faucet handles. Surprisingly, **the *floor* is often cleaner than the sink**—so now you know the best place in the kitchen to eat.

Hotel rooms are another source of woe for fecal fanatics. One study, conducted in the early 1990s, found that **a cheap hotel room had a lot more fecal bacteria in it than an expensive one.** Perhaps a reflection of the cleaning; perhaps of the caliber of guests.

One study found that 30 percent of all people didn't wash their hands after using a public bathroom—although 90 percent *claimed* they do. So do you really want to stick your hand in one of those **bowls of mints at the exits of some restaurants?** Did you ever wonder how many others who did that before you washed their hands before they left the bathroom?

No one has tested these mints for fecal matter, but one story, perhaps apocryphal, is that someone ran an ultraviolet light over a bowl to test for urine—and found it.

Other studies showed that **half of all homes surveyed had fecal material** in the washing machines, and **underwear contained as much as ten grams of fecal matter.** Washing didn't always help get rid of this, either, because most people do a load—a washing machine load, that is—along with other clothes, thereby spreading the fecal contamination around.

If you aren't yet on the verge of hiding in an expensive hotel room for the rest of your life, here are some other places fecal matter has been found:

- In one study, diarrhea-inducing *E. coli* was found on 10 percent of **coffee mugs;** another study found 50 percent of them to be contaminated.

- Between 7 and 42 percent of all paper money contained **"revolting bacteria."** (And everyone knows what those are!)

- One study found fecal matter on the **screen of an automated bank machine** (think of all the dirty fingers that touch those screens before you do).

- Microscopic crap droplets were found on **a headset in a 3-D movie theater.**

- People who touch a **pay phone** and then touch their faces afterwards are dialing for trouble.

ON THE LIGHTER SIDE

A study of cleanliness in movie theaters once found **vaginal bacteria on one of the seats.** God knows what the woman who was sitting there was wearing—or doing.

Cockroaches

Cockroaches were around before the dinosaurs—and will probably still be here long after humans are gone. They're so hardy that they can even live nine days without their heads before they starve to death.

Thus, the next humans to develop on what's left of this planet might arise from **cockroaches trillions of years from now.** They could even end up looking like … Linda Tripp?

For those who think nothing good ever comes from cockroaches, during the Vietnam War, the U.S. used cockroaches to detect farmers who were doubling as Communist guerrillas.

First, suspected Vietcong guerrilla meeting places were sprinkled with **synthetic female cockroach pheromones.**

Then, questionable Vietnamese farmers were made to walk slowly past cages containing male cockroaches. If a farmer had visited the meeting place earlier, the female scent on him would make the male cockroaches react.

According to *The Compleat Cockroach*, which provided most of the material in this section, in Brazil, there's **a species of cockroach that eats eyelashes,** usually those of young children while they are asleep. The hungry little insect is attracted to the minerals and moisture from the tear ducts—but that's not the only moisture they like to devour.

An entomologist was awakened one morning by a tickling sensation, only to find that a "cockroach's extended mouth parts were imbibing moist nutriment from my nostrils."

Cockroaches carry over forty different pathogens, which could potentially be transferred to humans. These include plague, pneumonia, typhoid fever, and possibly polio, hepatitis, and other diseases you don't want to get.

Here's some other info about this creature that is currently bugging us:

- An invention for **electrocuting cockroaches** was patented—by Thomas Edison.

- **Cockroach crap** is one of the causes of asthma.

- After food passes the cockroach's mouth parts, it travels backward and the food **mixes with spit** before they ingest it.

- Cockroaches have **teeth in their stomachs.**

ON THE LIGHTER SIDE

Although it may seem like a joke, **insect flatulence** may account for one-fifth of all the methane emissions on this planet. (Termites are also prodigious farters; indeed, dogs trained to sniff out termites are actually following their farts.)

Cockroaches are among the biggest contributors to global warming, since **they break wind every fifteen minutes.** Furthermore, they continue to release methane gas for eighteen hours after they die.

So, if you smell something funny after you spray your apartment, it may not be the insecticide.

Contests, Festivals, and Records, Weird

You think you have a bad boss? In a contest held by *Maxim* magazine to find out who had the worst boss, some agreed with the statement that their boss could be replaced by a hamster and no one would notice.

But one worker thought her boss stank the worst of them all because he was constantly **scratching his ass and sniffing the results**. And that stinks.

Most don't get a chance to enter contests that are quite so revealing, or to take part in festivals or try to break records that are, well, frankly weird. But there are exceptions.

Potty hearty: A toilet manufacturer is holding a contest for the **best potty-training photo**. The child who bowls the most people over with his or her on-the-john photo will receive a check for $25,000. Now, that's a lot of poop for a Kodak moment!

Stinky sneakers: The **National Rotten Sneaker Championship in Montpelier, Vermont,** offers the person with the foulest old sneakers a new pair—and a can of badly needed deodorant foot powder.

Residents of Talkeetna, Alaska, hold an annual **Moose Dropping Festival,** at which jewelry is fashioned from the animal's dung, swizzle sticks are decorated with moose droppings, and 750 gold-painted moose turds are dropped out of a helium balloon onto a field in which a giant X is painted. Whoever's gets closest to the X wins $1,000.

It was the best of slime, it was the worst of slime: Slimy Ivy League students recently competed in the first ever **slime tug-of-war.** The losers got dunked in a vat of the gooey stuff.

Elma, Washington, has an annual **slug festival** in which locals dress up as slugs and worm their way into slug races.

Seeing red: The *tomatina* festival in Bunol, Spain, has **the whole town throwing tomatoes at one another.**

The answer, my friends, is blowing in the wind—in Tracy, California. The question: Where is the Annual **Dry Bean Festival?** It's said to be a real gas.

ON THE LIGHTER SIDE

During the Great Arkansas Pig-Out, there's a contest called **Running of the Fat Guys.** Contestants weighing between 250 and 300 pounds run through three checkpoints, where they have to shovel down pizzas, cola, and Snickers bars.

Last year's winner clinched it when he ate a Snickers bar—wrapper and all.

Dismemberment

Losing parts of one's body is usually an accident, but in South Africa, there's a big market for people's eyes, breasts, brains, and genitals, which witch doctors use to prepare medicines for use in their ceremonies.

Some people are so eager to make a killing in this market that they're gladly making a literal killing, then scraping up the body's scraps for profit.

Most wanted body parts: **a girl's vulva—which is said to help productivity—and a man's testicles,** to enhance sexual strength and performance. What's a body to do?

Give these guys a hand (literally): In West Africa, Sierra Leone rebels have been **hacking off the limbs** of poor farmers and villagers. After all, it's hard for them to vote for someone else that way.

One refugee, whose hands were cut off, complained that he would never be able to use a toilet without help again.

The sound of one hand clapping: An English farmer had his right hand stuck in a hay-baling machine. As it continued to drag him in, he used the only thing around to save his life: his three-inch **penknife to hack off his trapped hand.**

You can't be too rich or too transplanted: Recently, a team of doctors **stitched a dead man's living hand** and forearm onto the arm of a forty-eight-year-old New Zealander. (Did they use elbow grease?)

Next? Probably the world's first face transplant. A body bank of pretty profiles for the rich and famous to put on like designer threads.

How were shrunken heads made? First they stole a head; then they sliced it down the back from the crown to the neck; peeled off the skin, as if they were taking off a glove; **cooked the skin;** sewed the incisions and other openings closed; tanned the head; and stuffed it.

The result was something to hang over the mantelpieces of their mud huts that was one-third its original size and pretty damned pissed.

(At least no one could ever accuse them of having swelled heads again.)

ON THE LIGHTER SIDE

Waiter! **There's a nose in my soup!** It's a snap now—literally—to put on a new face. A facial prosthesis has just been developed that snaps on, concealing missing noses, upper palates, and so on, that were lost to cancerous tumors and accidents.

The *Guinness World Records* TV show featured some sickening examples of people's new physiognomies. Still, it's an improvement over the old way. One patient complained that with his old-style fall-off prosthesis, he might lean over a bowl of hot soup and have his nose pop off. (Better soup than nuts.)

Enemas and High Colonics

Victim Victoria: The prim and proper **Victorians loved enemas**—mostly as medical treatment. A popular belief was that "autointoxication," or being poisoned by one's own feces, was a serious medical problem and the cause of a number of unwanted conditions and disturbing proclivities.

Getting rid of bodily wastes became such an obsessive interest on the part of mothers and nurses that the subject sometimes became mixed up in a child's mind with sex. Later in their lives, it became eroticized for them, and became part of what's euphemistically known as "Victorian discipline."

But enemas were not always a harmless folly. In those days, they were sometimes filled with turpentine, ox bile, and other worthless but potentially harmful substances.

Even today, people sometimes put unusual products in their enemas. Some people put **drinking alcohol in very diluted quantities in theirs.** This can be dangerous because of the speed of absorption, as well as the difficulty in getting rid of it if too much is inserted.

A bus driver in Budapest was prescribed a **paprika enema;** it led to such burning that he couldn't sit down to work for a month and sued for lost wages.

While **golden cocktails** involve drinking urine, with **golden enemas,** people use urine instead of water. The urine is often deposited directly in the partner's anus or vagina by urinating, or inserted into an enema bag and transferred to the other person that way. There are also **enema cocktails,** which involve some very close friends. (With friends like that, who needs enemas?)

The *New England Journal of Medicine* described a new disease called **"water skier's enema."** This occurs when the water skier lands in the water in a sitting position after skiing rapidly. The fall on the ass, in that position, and at that speed, with that impact, can lead to extreme cramps, followed by an intense need to defecate. When people do so, they have blood-tinted feces, but usually no problems later.

People who know they won't have easy access to a bathroom for a long time may take an enema. For example, one ardent fisherman, before going out for a weekend of fishing, holes up in a motel the night before to **flush his colon.** Then he doesn't have to spend a lot of time outside his boat looking for a place in the woods, and he has the added benefit of knowing he's not polluting the environment.

Public Enema Number Two: Over a ten-year period, the **"enema bandit,"** wearing a ski mask and carrying rubber tubing, sneaked up on dozens of women, pulled out a gun, tied the women up, and gave each an enema. Once, he managed to do it to a girl traveling on a train.

As it turns out, his enemas themselves weren't specifically against the law—who would think to put such a thing on the books? Fortunately, though, this Illinois man, who started doing this when he was in his twenties, stole not only his victims' dignity—one can imagine their embarrassment in reporting it later—but their cash. He was therefore successfully charged with theft. (Of money, that is, not of their excreta.)

Hi, Colonic: Although some celebrities swear by them—**Princess Di,** for example, had them regularly—the value of high colonics is questionable.

"We're talking about a high-tech enema here," says Cecil Adams of *The Straight Dope*, which always gives people exactly what the title promises. He says a high colonic accomplishes the same thing as a low-tech enema, except that "thanks to the lighted viewing tube, you get to watch the, uh, end result."

These worthless treatments also remove useful bacteria, can cause infection, and injure the sphincter and tissues. Sometimes they even kill people. Seven people died in the late '70s from a badly designed machine.

ON THE LIGHTER SIDE

An American artist named Keith Boadwee gives himself **paint enemas.** He puts paints of several different colors in his enema bag, uses it, then stands over a large canvas, turns his anus into a human spray gun, and lets loose. (The results compare favorably to a Jackson Pollock.)

Eyes

Eyes have been called the windows of the soul, but to some, they're somewhat less exalted. People with the fetish oculophilia really mean it when they say they *love* your eyes. Oculolinctus is licking eyeballs for sexual pleasure. Jeepers, creepers! Keep away from those peepers!

Eating human eyes is not a perversion, or for that matter even a known activity, but the abhorrent idea was given a lot of publicity when analyst Bobby Czyz tried to explain Mike Tyson's ear gobbling during boxing as follows: "In a world title fight, if I hit an opponent and his eye fell out of his head, **I'd eat [his eye]** before he could pick it up and put it back in."

Thankfully, Mr. Czyz is not scheduled for any eye-catching performances soon.

A Vancouver, B.C., graphic designer can **suck milk up his nose and squirt it out of his eye,** as well as blow bubbles—out of his eyes. (But why?)

A few animals have him beat, though. The Texas horned lizard ("horny toad") can increase the blood pressure in its head so it **can squirt blood out of its eye**—right into the face of its victim, as far as eight feet away.

And one type of snake can squirt venom into your eye from fifteen feet away. Eyeyeyeyeyey!

(See "Snakes, Eating or Biting You.")

ON THE LIGHTER SIDE

By mistake, a young man **dropped Krazy Glue into his eye** instead of saline solution when he put on his contacts, and glued his eyelids shut. Even worse, when he managed to find a phone and called the emergency hotline to tell them what happened, the operator said they got calls like that all the time!

Fart Artists and Igniters

Pull my finger, Beavis! Farts may often be a source of humor—and income—as proved by a Frenchman who packed audience halls in *fin de siècle* France, which, contrary to popular opinion, was as provincial and easily shocked as Victorian England.

Toward the end of the 1800s, **Joseph Pujol,** also known as Le Petomane—or **the manic farter**—became famous by playing a rather unconventional wind instrument. This he did while impeccably attired in a tuxedo, white stockings, and gloves, hardly projecting the appearance of someone who would then put out a candle a foot away, smoke a cigarette with a pipe attached to his rear, or imitate a dressmaker tearing calico.

He became so popular with this unconventional performance that he once gave a private showing for the Prince of Wales. When he died in 1945, at eighty-eight (his longevity possibly supporting those who say that holding in farts can hurt you), the Sorbonne, in Paris, even offered his family $10,000 to examine his body. Since the family knew what part of his body they wanted to examine, they turned them down.

Sensing which way the wind was blowing, a female attempted the same sort of performance. But Pujol went to court with her to prove she was a phony who was **concealing whistles under her skirts.** If Pujol demonstrated his talents in court during the trial, for once, a courtroom full of hot air may have been a reality rather than a metaphor.

Music to their rears: Today there are many amateurs who do this sort of thing, such as those who **pass Morse code messages out of their asses.** But people rarely make a living at this, even though some try, like a gaseous Japanese who farted 3,000 times in a row.

After Pujol and his immediate followers, such misbehavior was nothing, although the popularity of the Asian fartomaniac's act was indisputably bolstered by his finale. At that time, to the tune of a full orchestra (no doubt playing the 1812 Overture), a blowgun was inserted into his rectum and he fired darts at his audience.

The most famous professional "bottom burper" today is a British performer who calls himself **Mr. Methane** and performs **"rectal rumblings,"** such as playing the British national anthem (although Americans hear it as "My Country, 'Tis of Thee" and think he's performing for them).

On New Year's Eve, he also farts the countdown, and then plays "Auld Lang Syne." Unlike friendship, *this* is never forgotten.

Gone with the wind: There are two gases in farts that are flammable, and one (methane) is even used for heating stoves. That's why farts can flame, and a favorite game among jerks is to ignite their farts.

This can lead to singed hairs, second-degree burns, and a good time for a lot of young drunks.

Here are some variations of "going for the burn":

- **Lighting one's own farts.** The person holds the flame behind his ass while in a squatting position.

- **Fart ignition through underwear.** This presents potential dangers if one is wearing nylon or other synthetic shorts.

- **Fart-igniting contests and Olympic games.** One participant reported that at his college, "prizes for distance, brilliance, and overall artistic appeal" were awarded.

  Since it was an engineering school, "there was a great deal of preplanning for these contests, records kept, aggravating and mitigating conditions," and so on.

There have been a few cases in the medical literature of **patients' intestines exploding from cauterization during surgery.** In one famous American case, a doctor cauterized a rectal polyp, accidentally ignited a fart, and the explosion not only blew him back against the wall but ripped open six inches of the patient's colon.

In another instance, in England, a doctor removing hemorrhoids **had his eyebrows burned off when a fart caught fire.**

ON THE LIGHTER SIDE

The story of one unintended fart artist was reported in *Scientific American* a few years ago. This twenty-four-year-old man went to a Wales hospital complaining of weird crackling sounds coming from pockets of air trapped under his skin. The sounds came from all over his body, including his ass, "providing a **built-in whoopee-cushion effect.**"

It turns out that he had inflated a large number of balloons for a party earlier that day. His vigorous blowing had ruptured some of his alveoli, causing this effect.

Farters, Famous

Portrait of the pervert as a young man: Any number of scatological lex-icographers, from Aristophanes through Petronius, Boccaccio, Rabelais, and Chaucer, have dealt smelly epithets to that invisible but noisy little fart. But can a fart be art? And if it's *really* scatological, should the writing be excised into eternity, as most prudes would no doubt wish to do to the following paragraph?

> A little brown stain on the seat of your white drawers ... a sudden immodest noise made by your behind and then a bad smell slowly curling up out of your backside. **I hope Nora will let off no end of farts in my face** so that I may know of their smell also.

One wonders what sort of mind could emit such a fit of literary flatulence, and whether this example has any artistic merit. (Hey, it's easy to write that stuff within a self-admittedly sleazy volume with no pretensions whatever.)

But should a government ever fund, or even tolerate, such repugnant outbursts, and the "artists" behind them? And should people be allowed to read them?

Perhaps it's time to expose the sleazemonger who wrote this, to reveal his name so he can be treated as he deserves.

His name is James Joyce. Among his many ripping good tales, he wrote *Finnegans Wake, Portrait of the Artist as a Young Man*—and *Ulysses*, which many consider to be the greatest novel ever written.

Perhaps the world would have been different if Beano had been around in the '20s. It turns out that **Adolf Hitler** suffered from **chronic flatu-lence,** a condition probably not helped by his indulgence in pulverized bull testicles, Bavarian sausages, game pie, and baby pigeons, even though he was widely believed to be a vegetarian.

One researcher thinks that Hitler's farting may have changed his personality, and therefore the world. Hitler took extremely large amounts of pills for his excruciating cramps. These pills contained strychnine and belladonna, which can cause hallucinations, violence, and so on.

It's not only historical figures whose eructation habits and interests have become known to us. **Jennifer Aniston,** who has admitted that she's **obsessed with farts,** is quoted in *Stupid Celebrities* as saying that the best way to break the ice on a first date is to just fart away.

She also told *Us* magazine that she got interested in this subject when she got **turned on to a farting tape,** and also discovered a product called **Fart in a Can.** She would squirt this between takes and break up the crew, until the cast of *Friends* took the gadget away from her.

After all, friends don't let friends fart.

Rap fartists, er, artists: Will Smith attributes his success to a farting product. Without it, he says, he might never have become a famous rapper. According to *Wireless Flash,* Will's rap partner, Jeff, started **spraying "fart spray" around.** Will was the only other person who thought it was funny—so it brought the two of them together.

Well, hello, Dali! The painter **Salvador Dali** was another flatulator—also a nut who wore a perfume of fish glue and cow dung—which are two of many interesting facts in *The Re/Search Guide to Bodily Fluids,* which contains information most books don't touch upon (except for this one, of course).

The author revealed that Dali "was capable of putting out a candle at a distance of two yards simply by bending over in a certain way," and that he also **"played pool with his farts."**

Another fact unearthed in this book is that **Thomas Edison** fed a playmate large doses of laxatives to see if his friend could fly through the air, **propelled by his own flatus.**

What a gas: **Robert Mitchum,** an old-time movie star, told his future wife, "Stick with me, kid, and you'll be **farting through silk."**

One infamous farter: Some years ago, on Fire Island, New York, a house burglar hiding in a closet was caught as a result of **an untimely escape—from his ass,** not from the house.

ON THE LIGHTER SIDE

An unknown writer gained ephemeral fame by winning a "worst possible opening line for a book" contest. His entry: "As a scientist, Throckmorton knew that if he were ever to **break wind in the sound chamber,** he would never hear the end of it."

Farting Facts

Academics have failed to overcome their reputation for being gasbags by conducting studies on this room-clearing phenomenon—some by a researcher with the unfortunate name of Colin Leakey—some using fartometers and fartograms, and some plain old sniffers wearing "gas masks."

Here are some of the more interesting findings these fart smellers—ah, smart fellers—have learned:

- Rates vary, but generally most **people fart more than ten and fewer than twenty times** each day. The quantity is said to be enough to blow up one small balloon.

- Each volley of farts consists of about 9 percent carbon dioxide and 7 percent methane, two gases that **contribute to global warming.**

- The **world's greatest contemporary farter** is said to be an eleven-year-old who farted 217 times in five minutes on a radio call-in show.

- Meat contains many chemicals that cause **the smelliest farts,** but the all-time winner of any sniff tests may be the cowpea. One man wrote that cowpeas lead to indigestion, diarrhea, vomiting, increased belching, halitosis, offensive stool, flatulence, constipation, abdominal discomfort and sleepiness, "which raises the question as to why they haven't become more popular than they are."

- People who think their families stink may be right. **Flatulence runs in families,** because they have a tendency to harbor similar intestinal parasites, along with an inclination to eat the same types of foods.

- **Farts can actually be seen on some x-rays.**

- It has been jokingly pointed out that the difference between men's and women's flatulating habits is that women are less likely than guys to congratulate each other on their gas eruptions.

  One serious study on the differences between the sexes concerning their eructation habits found that when fed the exact same food, **women have more concentrated gas than men,** or "a greater odor intensity."

- In other words, even when they eat the same thing and produce the same amount of gas, **women's farts smell worse.** One humorist wrote that the fact that men and women fart equally means "a lot of women owe a lot of apologies to a lot of dogs."

- Although teenagers may fart a lot because of their unfortunate diet, the **older you get the more you fart,** because **your bowels become less elastic.** The amount of gas the body produces, however, remains the same if the diet does.

- A half-serious letter to the editor of the *New England Journal of Medicine* pointed out that **"the 'slider' (the crowded-elevator type) lasts longer**. . . . The open-sphincter, or the 'pooh,' type is of a higher temperature and is more aromatic than the 'slider.' . . . The tighter the sphincter, the higher the pitch and the less the resonance."

- It is known that escaping gas from a corpse sometimes make it sound as if someone is **farting after death.** One man wrote to *Bizarre* magazine—an extraordinarily interesting magazine that should be the bible of every disgustingness fan—that he's eating fruits and vegetables so he can go out with a bang when he dies. He added that his mother, a nurse, said that skinny people made the loudest farts.

The gas you pass: A number of interesting facts about farting come from a fascinating new book titled *Who Cut the Cheese? A Cultural History of Farting*:

- Less than 1 percent of a fart is made up of the **chemicals that stink,** but they're so pungent that people can smell them at levels of 1 part in 100 million.

- Farts are created mostly by *E. coli* and other bacteria that are **microfarting** inside of you.

- The **temperature of your fart** is 98.6 degrees, the same as your body should be.

- Farts **have been clocked at 10 feet per second,** which is pretty fast.

- Ten percent of the American public is plagued by **farting too much.** So you see, it's not just your uncle Charlie.

❁

Tooting their own horn: The Yanomami, an Indian tribe in South America, **use farting as a greeting.** (If they used it as a farewell, they could say "Farting is such sweet sorrow.")

ON THE LIGHTER SIDE

Discovery magazine once presented the joking comment that flatulence was the way the body got rid of unwanted gases, the intestines of unwanted pressure, "and crowded theater rows of unwanted strangers."

Farting, Products Related to

Many farting items intended to become the "butts" of jokes are available, sold by companies with names like **Farty Pants** and entrepreneurs with names like **Joe Stinker,** who sell a wide array of products for those who think trouser tornadoes are a real toot. For example:

- **Farting/talking wristwatches.** Mr. Tooty tells you the time of day and then lets one rip. It also works as an alarm clock: "Good Morning. Rise and —" at which point an appropriate sound is made.

- **Jurassic Fart T-shirts** feature a picture of a squatting dinosaur.

- **"Flatology 101 T-shirts"** describe school courses in farting, such as the **"Seven Habits of Highly Flatulent People."**

- **"The America Flatulators,"** and other "rip-roaring videos," are guaranteed to leave you "gasping for air," the promoters promise.

- **"Pull My Finger"** makes the claim that "no fake or synthesized sounds were used in this **disgusting thirty-minute compilation."**

- **Whoopee cushions.** Incidentally, actress **Whoopi Goldberg** admits that she got her nickname because she farted so much as a child; she had sort of a built-in whoopee cushion.

- **Remote-controlled farting machines** allow the immature to embarrass others with up to four different fart sounds made from a distance, so that people will think the victim is the farter.

- **Fart Spray,** advertised as "the smell of farts at your fingertips," is a product that's nothing to sniff at.

- Novelty **matchbooks to light your farts,** for those who are into advanced pyroflatulence.

- **A fart whistle.** (If you don't want these people around, just whistle.)

Jack the Ripper: But not all these products are jokes. Those with chronic flatus who can't control their eructations have not found life to be a breeze. For those unfortunates, **flatulence filter products** have been developed.

These have been scientifically (if amusingly) tested by giving subjects pinto beans and lactulose the night before, and then putting them into airtight Mylar underpants, connected by an exhaust tube to a charcoal cushion.

The best known flatulence filter is called a **Toot Trapper.** It's a cushion containing activated charcoal. (Activated carbon technology, incidentally, was developed to protect troops from nerve gas attacks, but, of course, that is a different kind of gas.)

Studies showed that the Toot Trapper captured 90 percent of the odor. Interestingly, just sitting on a dummy cushion absorbed 40 percent of the flatulence smells.

Similar products are the **Ass Mask,** which the manufacturer calls a **"fart disabler,"** and the **Fart Filter,** advertised as being effective on "dog farts, toots or poots, windys, squeakers, sonic boom farts, percolating farts, coughing or laughing farts, and finally the S.B.D. farts (silent but deadly)."

ON THE LIGHTER SIDE

Conan O'Brien tells us, "a toy company announced that it's coming out with **a brand-new virtual pet that eats, sleeps, burps, and passes gas.** Apparently, it was designed to show young women what it's like to be married."

Foot Fetishism

Some men get a kick out of women's feet; indeed, many people no longer think it's all that disgusting. But the media generally act as if it is, and it invariably damages a person's reputation if it comes out that they're into feet.

For example, **Dick Morris,** former advisor (and then turncoat enemy) of priapic President **Bill Clinton,** was outed and briefly reviled for **sucking the toes of prostitutes**. Not only that, but he did it while on the White House payroll, even while talking to the President—who was probably doing worse at the time.

People have eroticized feet throughout the centuries, and in many cultures, women would sooner have showed their sex organs than their tootsies. Roman women even put weights in their togas so their feet wouldn't show.

According to *The Odd Index*, in Laos, **a woman can't show her toes in public,** and there's a law on the books in China that if some heel looks at the bare feet of another man's wife, the offended husband is supposed to kill him.

Sock it to me: Occasionally, a man is **obsessed with socks** instead of feet, and the *Mainichi Daily News* in Tokyo last year reported the case of a man who became so furious that some woman's socks were loose around her ankles that he "assaulted her"—by rubbing his spit in her hair.

He was quoted in *News of the Weird* as saying, "When I saw those socks I just went crazy." (But maybe he was just trying to save this woman's sole.)

I want to hold your . . . socks? A more ridiculous case, in England, was reported in *Fortean Times:* Two men enticed 15,000 men—including two policemen and a traffic warden—into **giving them their smelly old socks.** The donors believed they were helping to raise money for a cancer charity.

The two also paid men to sit with their feet in one of their faces, while the partner photographed this, ahem, orgy. Questions about their activities arose after they had some film developed.

When the police came to the apartment, they found over 10,000 pairs of socks "all over the furniture, hanging from the lampshades, and even in the microwave, frying pan, and cooker."

The court socked it to them with a year-and-a-half jail sentence.

Speaking of high smell content, here's a story that should be titled "The Smell of De-Feet." In California, when a policeman stopped a driver who wasn't wearing a seat belt, the driver's excuse was that he wanted to smell his feet!

But those who are into this type of kink usually want to smell *other people's* feet. For example, one man used to call strangers and simply ask them one question: **"Do your feet stink?"**

The judge apparently thought this harassment stank and sent him back to prison, where he had already served a sentence for the same behavior.

Once in a while, someone is into toenails, such as the man, dubbed **"Leonardo da Toenail,"** who painted the toenails of women as they studied. That seems somewhat harmless, but one twenty-four-year-old was arrested in California for using a black pen to **color women's toenails.** What was the difference? He sneaked into their homes to do it, and painted their toenails while they slept.

ON THE LIGHTER SIDE

A Tory minister in England, instead of putting his foot in his own mouth, got caught putting *someone else's* foot in his mouth. When he was dismissed, one tabloid gleefully crowed: "Toe Job, No Job."

Freaks, Man-Made and Phony

It's horrible to think that throughout history, people have been deliberately deformed—even "created"—as freaks. But it's true. For example, in the decadent late Roman Empire, there was a low trend among the upper classes of having at least one dwarf among their servants. When the natural supply ran out, they developed a method of producing more. They deprived young children of food (except for brandy), and **kept them almost entirely submerged in alcohol to shrink them.** (Strictly bottom-shelf material.)

In ancient China, where dwarves were also prized, they had to be manufactured. They placed these poor children in **topless and bottomless vases,** constricting the growth of their torsos.

Not just another pretty face: In Paris in the 1700s, physicians sometimes performed a horribly painful operation called **a denatsate, which extended the mouth with slits cut from the corners of the lips to the ears.** The teeth were left in place, but the gums and nose were removed, creating **a sickening grin and a gaping hole.** According to *Morbid Fact du Jour,* people would pay the skull-faced beggar just to get him out of their sight.

Today, it's been reported that in Gujrat, Pakistan, there are as many as 10,000 hideous sexless mute retarded **rat children who are used for begging.** These freaks were created by **placing their heads in iron vases** when they were very young. The unfortunate children then developed sloped-back foreheads, elongated hands, pointy noses, and slanted eyes.

The children are said to be inherently gentle, but they've been trained to attack people who don't give them money. They're worked like slaves, and their owners work them fast, because their average life expectancy isn't even thirty years.

A kiss is just a (disgusting) kiss. In parts of Zaire, **really big lips are considered beautiful.** So much so that female babies' lips are slit and wooden disks are inserted into them. By the time these women have matured, so have their lips—to a (to us) disgusting ten inches or more.

They've got a good point: Instead of getting swelled heads, a certain African tribe **binds the heads** of their young to produce small and pointed heads, which they believe to be beautiful.

ON THE LIGHTER SIDE

Sideshow acts were often fraudulent, and Pasqual Pinon, who was popular in the early 1900s, had a tumor growing on top of his head outfitted with facial features. He then billed himself as the **"Two-Headed Mexican."**

As if that weren't bad enough, William Durks, **"The Man with Three Eyes,"** had a phony third eye painted onto his severe cleft palate. (Beauty is in the lips of the beholder.)

Freaks, Natural

A singer once said that short people didn't deserve to live, and one Roman emperor, in the year 192, felt the same way. He collected all the **dwarves, cripples, and freaks,** and put them together in the famed Coliseum. They were given meat cleavers, and they fought like tigers until none of them were left.

The freaks that have most fascinated people were those with two heads, who invariably proved that two heads *weren't* better than one. Edward Mordrake was born with **another face on the back of his head.** It was said to be a girl, who couldn't speak or eat (are they sure it was a girl?), but her eyes moved and she could cry.

So could Mr. Mordrake. He begged doctors to remove his "devil," but none would or could in those days. He finally killed her—by committing suicide at the age of twenty-three.

Another two-headed boy only lived to the age of four before dying of a cobra bite. **His second head had a brain,** whose emotional responses were different from his. Except, one imagines, when the first was bitten by the snake.

Still another two-headed boy was born in Bengal in 1783. When the second head was **given a female breast, it attempted to nurse.** But then, who wouldn't?

For some, the head or body is less developed. According to the website mrshowbiz.com, **Andy Garcia** was born with his twin attached to his shoulder. The "fetus," which was no bigger than a tennis ball, had to be removed by surgeons right after Andy's birth in Cuba in 1956.

For this "accomplishment" he was awarded a mention in the *Guinness Book of World Records* as the Most Successful Conjoined Twin of Modern Times.

Although not quite the victim of an encapsulated birth, something was, ah, queer about **Liberace** from the very start. He weighed 13 pounds at birth, and he was one of twins—the other was a skeletal child who didn't survive birth.

Even odder, Liberace later **had his lover reconstructed by plastic surgery** to make him look as his twin would have looked had he lived. In other words, made to look like him.

Anne Boleyn had six fingers and three breasts. Henry VIII's third wife had the beginnings of a sixth digit on one of her hands. The women at court hated her and, to embarrass her, would invite her to play cards. This was an underhanded trick, since ladies always had to remove their gloves when playing cards.

If the women of the court had really wanted to get under her skin, they would have asked her to take off her blouse. She also had a vestigial nipple, the start of a third breast—a fact that would have titillated her enemies had her secret been known to them.

A man born in 1617 carried a twin with head, trunk, arms, and one leg inside him. This parasitic **twin would often be asleep while the man was awake**—which must have been hard to explain if his "twin" started snoring.

Petrifying story: A woman who died at ninety-two was found to have **been carrying her dead baby—long since calcified—for sixty years.** Now there's a mama's boy!

All humans have tails in the sixth week of gestation, but the tail bails out during the seven or eighth week. Usually. There are over **160 cases of tailed humans** in the medical literature—the latest as recent as 1998.

The longest appendages were a foot in length, and Marco Polo described some that were 7 to 10 inches, were sensitive, and had the same mobility as an elephant's trunk.

Some people can wag them and move them, but not far enough to sit down and "read" their own tall tails.

A few people have also made money out of them, like the 1880s sideshow attraction, **"Lady with a Mane"** who had a "horse tail" along her back.

ON THE LIGHTER SIDE

Some would rather bite than fight. A three-foot dwarf in Germany got in trouble when he became so **enraged at the big-butted passengers** squeezing up against him on a train, pushing a heaping serving of seat meat into his mouth with every stop, that he literally took a bite for small people's rights—right out of their asses.

Infections, Yeast

Someone wrote to "Ask Bizarre" to ask about yeast feasts; *Bizarre* suggested people check out the feminist-run yeast infection home page and "detail what it's like to walk around miserable for days **with disgusting slime dribbling down between your legs.**"

But yeast infections aren't only fun for the females. "Ask Bizarre" pointed out that "gays and other back-door bandits" sometimes get thrush around the anus, and that there's a rare oral version of this too.

Do home remedies work? "The last girl we know who tried to banish thrush by **shoving a clove of garlic up her whatsit** got it stuck and couldn't persuade her boyfriend to give her oral sex for a month."

An Internet site on male yeast infections got into the act, pointing out that **men with large foreskins are more likely to get yeast infections,** because there's smegma there for the yeast to feast on. The smegma "usually shows up after some days of hefty wanking and dubious hygiene as a reddish rash. . . . Watch as the rash turns into little red sores that'll itch more and more," they wrote cheerfully.

ON THE LIGHTER SIDE

Another poster said that before soap was invented, "The cure [for yeast infections] was to **hold the foreskin closed when pissing** until it was bloated with piss, and then let fly all over yourself and the toilet. Stuff in the urine should then clean out the yeast." (Not to mention everybody in the men's room.)

Kissing and Aphrodisiacs

We think of kissing as romantic and a sexual turn-on, but the mouth contains over 250 different types of bacteria. A children's book titled *Grossology Begins at Home* decided to teach kids while they were still young and impressionable just how vile kissing really was by including an essay in the book titled **"Ten Reasons Why You Shouldn't Kiss Anyone Except Your Dog"**:

- **One-hundred billion critters** live in a human mouth.
- **Fungus** grows in the oral cavity.
- **White blood cells** from someone else's spit attack your mouth.
- Kissing transfers tiny amounts of **leftover food** (sometimes from days before).
- **Spit contains urine.**

Other societies have also made sure people didn't find kissing too arousing, at least if they were kissing someone they weren't supposed to touch. An Assyrian law table, written in 1450 B.C., said that if a man kissed the wife of another citizen, his lower lip should be drawn along the edge of an axe blade and cut off.

Of course, kissing isn't the only turn-on, and some of the concoctions people have used as alleged aphrodisiacs sound pretty nauseating to us now. For example, one favorite recipe called for **the semen of virile men to be mixed with the excrement of hawks.** This "delicacy" was then turned into a pellet so it could be easily eaten.

Animals (and their droppings and parts) have been used for centuries as alleged aphrodisiacs, either ingested or placed on the cock, although it's hard to see why people thought some of the following would actually turn them on:

- **Toad excrement** in eighteenth-century France.
- **Pigeon dung and snail excrement** in medieval England.
- **Sheep's eyelid** marinated in hot tea.
- **Dolphin and chicken testicles.**

Inappropriate parts of animals are still sometimes used, well, inappropriately. A recent week-long conference in India, analyzing a variety of supposed turn-ons, included a discussion of the value of **whale poop as an aphrodisiac.** (They never got around the difficulty of finding volunteers to test this.)

Rotten apples: In Elizabethan England, one way young lovers kept each other hot and bothered was by passing **"love apples"** to each other. These were skinned apples that the men and women **kept in their armpits** to soak up their fragrance. Then they would give the apples to their lovers, who would carry them around, inhaling their scent whenever their hearts desired.

A **"prostate warmer,"** technically called a G-H-R Electric Thermitis Dilator, was once touted as a device to rejuvenate the sex drive. But it certainly wouldn't have carried an Underwriters' Laboratories seal of approval. You plugged it into an electrical socket, shoved it where electricity should never go, and prayed that you had good medical insurance.

ON THE LIGHTER SIDE

Last year, a chef in France offered a **"Viagra Menu,"** boasting such delicacies as Beef Piccata—in Viagra. One hopes that no one at the end of the meal said anything like "Will everyone at the table please rise?"

Masturbation

*P*lease, *mother, I'd rather do it myself:* A few **names for masturbation** include choking the bald guy till he pukes, freeing Willy, brushing the beaver, and Jocelyn Eldering.

A popular way to do it—with a piece of liver—was described in the best-selling *Portnoy's Complaint* by Philip Roth, leading writer Jacqueline Susann to say of Roth, "I've never met him, but I wouldn't shake his hand."

But telling large numbers of people exactly how to use a slab of liver had to wait until the Internet came along. **"Wrap the liver around your cock,** perhaps fasten it with rubber bands and get wanking," wrote a man who also recommended "lard fucking" and "fruit fucking." (For "the bumhole," he mentioned electric toothbrushes and a "butt harp.")

One twenty-seven-year-old man in Illinois, who chose a vegetable instead of liver for gratification, later regretted his choice of sex partner when he was supposedly caught **masturbating into a pumpkin** at 11:38 on a Friday night.

A policeman approached him and asked, "Excuse me, sir, but do you realize that you're screwing a pumpkin?"

Newspapers reported that he replied, "A pumpkin? Is it midnight already?"

Masturbation, or Sex with the One(s) You Love: Almost every college has stories about circle jerks. A group of **students sit in a circle, jerk off, and see who can come first.**

Sometimes the lights are off, and all but one of the men just make soft sounds by rubbing their hands together. When the "victim" starts to come, they turn on the light, and he discovers that he's the only one actually doing some gherkin jerkin'.

Other popular variations of such games include **ejaculating onto food** (favorites are soggy biscuits, white bread, chocolate pudding, etc.). The last person to come has to eat it.

A really bizarre way to pull your pud with another is called docking. One partner pulls his foreskin back, and the other **stretches his foreskin over the other's man's penis.** One foreskin then covers the two wieners and both can be jerked off at once. (This could bring a whole new meaning to all the docking sequences in *Star Trek*, not to mention those "docking maneuvers" our astronauts practice with the Russians!)

Someone also recently invented a kind of harness underwear that slings the prick away from a man's thighs, thereby supposedly **reducing the premature ejaculation** that comes from constantly stimulating Mr. Happy.

No one understands why it would work, but long lines of people are ready to try it.

Penis Power: Although **chimpanzees can blow themselves**—and often do—according to the *Kinsey Report*, only two or three out of a thousand **men can lick their own wangs.** Which doesn't stop the rest from checking at least once in their life to see whether they're one of the lucky few.

Brenda Love's incredible *Encyclopedia of Unusual Sexual Practices* describes the best position for a lucky man to perform auto-fellatio. He sits upside down on a couch with his head and shoulders resting on the bottom cushion, so that **his penis is in front of his mouth.**

She writes that some men are able to ejaculate into their own mouths. One teenager who accomplished this said most of the sensation is in the mouth rather than the phallus. (And most of the profit is made by the chiropractors who have to straighten these people out afterwards.)

Even more remarkable, if one is so inclined—actually, to do this right you have to be *reclined*—is something called autopederasty. This rather difficult act is performed by the rare few who can (and wish to) **insert their own penises into their asses,** thereby enabling them literally to have their heads up their asses.

A **nun lost a perfume bottle** up her vagina, presumably because she was using it to masturbate. (This is better than using a candle, wick in and wick out.)

Things don't necessarily go better with Coke. Coke bottles were once **popular masturbation items,** although not necessarily good ones. Occasionally, a vacuum formed, sucking in the Real Thing, and the bottle then had to be surgically removed.

The handle of a broom reached one woman's vagina after entering through her ass; obviously she'd been masturbating with it, but she said it all happened when she fell down the stairs.

ON THE LIGHTER SIDE

Howard Stern quipped, "My mother would always say, 'What happened to all the Kleenex?' and I had to pretend I had a cold."

Masturbation, Stopping It

Where there's fun, there have always been people trying to stop it. Especially in the punishment-drenched ancient days. For example, the Talmud forbids men to **hold their penises while urinating** (presumably because it might result in a Phil Roth novel).

Hebrew touchiness is also reflected in such draconian laws as the old Judaic one that declared that **masturbation should be punished by death.** (According to modern Jewish law, masturbation is now punished by Jewish mothers.)

Even today, the penalty for masturbation in Indonesia is said to be decapitation. Can't say it wouldn't stop it.

Cereal killers: No less an "authority" than John Kellogg, brother of the famous cereal king who invented corn flakes, suggested **blistering and irritating the clitoris,** and/or removing it entirely, as a cure for female masturbation and nymphomania.

Kellogg also recommended that the dry cereal be taken not only by mouth but as an enema! Either way, he said, it would work "as a bland alternative . . . which . . . would help patients **keep their hands off their genitals,**" according to *History Laid Bare*.

More drastically, Kellogg recommended a **clitoridectomy to cure masturbation.** In one case, it was performed on a girl of about eight who had become "addicted to the vice." This barbaric operation was performed in the U.S. as recently as fifty years ago, on a five-year-old girl to "cure" her of masturbation.

Women weren't the only ones to undergo terrible treatments in an attempt to stop people from doing what comes even more naturally.

Within the last 100 years, **cures for male masturbation have included blistering and cauterizing the penis** with red mercury ointment.

As recently as 100 years ago, in Texas, there was even a case of amputation to stop masturbation. It probably worked, too, just as cutting off a person's toes would permanently end the problem of ingrown toenails or bad dancing.

ON THE LIGHTER SIDE

A simple way to stop some masturbation was resorted to in some harems when it was discovered that women were **putting cucumbers up themselves to masturbate.**

They insisted that all cucumbers be sliced before they were presented to the horny harem women. And that sure put them in a pickle!

Menstruation

Back in the 1800s, when everything stank and everyone loved it, many found menstrual odors to be sexually intoxicating, and a woman coming of age was proud of it. In some countries, families **hung the bloody sheets,** showing proof of a woman's first period, out the window.

Men sometimes sniffed and **drank menstrual blood as an aphrodisiac.** Some women took their menstrual blood and **mixed it into their husband's food or drink,** in the belief that it would make their husbands more amorous toward them.

Welcome to womanhood: The **first period** was more often reviled than revered, and women were frequently treated harshly during their menses. In one South American tribe, as soon as a girl exuded her first drop of blood, she was **sewn up in a hammock,** with only a tiny opening allowing her to breathe.

Then the hammock was suspended over a smoky fire for days in order to purify her—if it didn't kill her.

It was not only the women who suffered during the menses. In some New Mexican tribes, a man couldn't approach his wife for sex for one week after she completed her period. If he did, and it was discovered, he could be put to death.

Even dogs were said to suffer from contact with a woman on the rag. An old wives' tale has it that **dogs that lap up menstrual blood go mad,** and if they bite a person after drinking it, the bite may kill the human.

Menstruation is still considered so unclean in many places that in India, for instance, there are signs outside of temples saying that a **menstruating woman cannot enter.** Even if the woman's brother is getting married, she may not be able to attend the wedding if she's bleeding.

It could be worse—and has been. There were times in Indian history when a woman who was having her period when her husband died could be burned alive. (Now they don't need an excuse to do that to a woman.)

❧

Women living close to each other, such as roommates, often have the onset of their periods at the same time. To prove that the odors of one woman could influence the menstrual cycle of another, in a classic experiment, the pheromones of women during their periods were extracted by **putting pads under their armpits for a day.**

Then these pads were rubbed on the other women's upper lips—which did indeed effect the start of their cycle.

❧

Marilyn Monroe apparently didn't mind airing her dirty linen, literally, according to her former seamstress and special confidante Lena Pepitone, who wrote one of the first tell-all books about her, *Marilyn Monroe Confidential: An Intimate Personal Account.*

She says that when Marilyn got her period, she didn't wear any sanitary protection. She bled right onto her sheets and let others clean up the bloody mess.

❧

There have been occasional reports of **menstruating men:**

- A man in the 1700s **supposedly menstruated a couple of days each month through his penis.**

- Another man was reported to have **menstruated—through his nose.**

- Men in one New Guinea tribe cut their johnsons regularly to make them bleed as if they were having periods.

ON THE LIGHTER SIDE

Several years ago, when the First Women's Bank first opened, the joke was going around that the bank was open seven days a week—except for three days each month, when it closed down because of cramps.

Monkey Brains, Eating of

In many parts of Asia today, monkey brains are considered not only a delicacy but an aphrodisiac. The current favored method of monkey-eating in various Southeast Asian countries is to force the monkey to drink alcohol until it's unconscious. Then, while it's alive, its brains are scooped out and eaten.

A harsher earlier method was detailed in a fascinating book called *Who Needs a Road?*—the story of the world's longest auto expedition, taken by two adventurers. "The waiter brought out a live monkey in a basket. The monkey was still jabbering away happily as the waiter slipped him under the table and brought his head up through the hole in the center.

"Then, with a practiced chop . . . **he cut off the top of the monkey's head,** flipping it over to expose the brain, gray and moist and still pulsating inside . . . [and then] demonstrat[ed] the proper technique for scooping out pieces of brain with a demitasse spoon and exhorting us to eat while it was still warm."

ON THE LIGHTER SIDE

This is a bit hard to swallow, but there's a dish called **Three Screams Delight** in which newborn mice, rats, or hamsters are served live.

- ◉ The first scream is when the fork is stuck in.
- ◉ The second comes from dipping it in the sauce.
- ◉ And the third comes when you bite it.

Museums, Records, and Collections, Tasteless

Museums are supposed to be institutions of learning, but one wonders what is learned from some of them. For example, the Mutter Museum of Philadelphia has the **cancerous tissue from the jaw of President Grover Cleveland and the joined livers of the original Siamese twins.**

The Museum of Death in San Diego has a **serial killer art gallery,** with the bloodstained shirt of someone who died in the electric chair, and the hand of a schizophrenic who cut it off, thinking it was possessed by the devil.

There's a museum on the history of urology that features an exhibit on **"Stone Surgery through the Ages."** Think kidney stones are painful today? To get them out years ago, "doctors" ripped open the victim's bladder, often leaving the patients to bleed to death. (At least they got the stones out!)

Here's looking at you, kid: The Kunsthal Gallery in Rotterdam exhibits such Ripleyesque items as a preserved deformed baby with one eye and **Siamese twin fetuses** joined at the chest and floating in a jar of formaldehyde.

A few other weird museums to visit:

- In Maryland, there's a **Museum of Menstruation.**
- The Madison (Wisconsin) **Museum of Bathroom Tissue** contains 3,000 rolls of toilet paper.
- Don't be bugged about not being cultured. Visit Sweden's **mosquito museum.**

- The **Museum of Dentistry** features a jukebox shaped like a giant maw.
- There's a **cockroach museum** in Plano, Texas.

Going to pot: In Munich there's a collection of over **2,000 chamber pots,** including musical ones. One made during World War II has Hitler's face painted on the bottom of it. Sieg heil—right in the Fuhrer's face.

One man has collected over 500 airsickness bags and displays photos of many of them—including what looks like a used Air India bag.

The whole tooth and nothing but: Someone collected **28,000 rotting teeth** and turned them into a sculpture of sorts in China. (But why go to China to see 28,000 rotting teeth when Arkansas is so much closer?)

ON THE LIGHTER SIDE

Art for tart's sake. A museum in Belgium exhibited a series of collages featuring respected royal figures in pornographic images, a comic book hero sodomizing his dog, and **underwear of the rich and famous,** which he solicited from singers, actors, and other famous folks. (The Belgians should stick to chocolate.)

Nipples

American television has agonized for decades over the parts of the breast it may decently allow to be seen, at times horrified by the idea of cleavage, and at other times petrified lest the flesh around the nipple be seen. Now TV seems to tolerate anything but the naked nipple itself, though erect nipples occasionally peep enticingly through white cotton or silk in the racier programs.

Of course, one isn't supposed to have more than two of them—nipples, that is—although **Mark Wahlberg** (Marky Mark) **has three nipples.** The reason you don't see it—and probably didn't know about it unless you heard him talking about it on the *Howard Stern* show—is that it was airbrushed out in his famous Calvin Klein underwear ads.

Lorne Greene surely didn't want to have his nipples pierced, but when he was on "Lorne Greene's Wild Kingdom," one of his guests did it for him anyway. **An alligator bit off one of his nipples** while he was hosting his popular animal show.

Here's an udderly ridiculous story. One California woman said she could still produce milk four years after giving birth—and showed off this useless skill to the poor souls trying to have a peaceful lunch at a pizza parlor, without her spritzing and mooing them.

When the police arrived, **she squirted the sergeant in the face with milk.** According to *Stupid Sex*, she had a history of "unauthorized squirting." This included one case in which she squirted milk at a man while shouting: "Bet you can't do this, sonny!"

In the late 1890s, **bosom rings** came into fashion. These rings were inserted through the nipple, and some women wore one on each side, linking them together with decorative chains.

The fashion died out after people began to think the rings were revolting, but now it's coming back, even though most people still think it's vile. What's old is nude again.

According to *Sex Chronicles*, in the Assini region of Africa, very **large nipples** were considered sexy, so girls submitted to painful techniques to achieve these saucer-sized nipples. They encouraged the larvae of insects to attack their nipples, or poured substances on them to irritate the skin, causing the nipples to swell.

In the Middle Ages, having a **third nipple** identified a person as a witch, since the Devil supposedly sucked it. That really sucked, because people who were thought to be witches were put to death.

ON THE LIGHTER SIDE

Why do Jehovah's Witnesses have **inverted nipples?** From people poking them in the chest, saying, "Get the fuck off my porch!"

Peeing in Public

In the 1700s and 1800s, wealthy men often carried bottomless canes, wide enough so they could stick Uncle Dick into it and (somewhat discreetly) go when nature called.

As for women, one reason they wore long puffy dresses was so **they could pee easily** without anyone noticing them. After voiding their bladders, they would just walk away, leaving an odiferous trail behind them.

It was also said that those **long dresses enabled them to fart freely,** and the scent couldn't escape from its corseted cage.

Royal flush: During interminable court banquets, chamberpots were discreetly placed under the dinner tables so the guests could relieve themselves. According to *An Underground Education,* when **Anne Boleyn** was crowned queen, two maids were hidden under the banquet table. One was assigned to hold the pot; the other, a lace handkerchief.

Lesser nobility were given sponges.

Men like to find **unusual places to pee,** such as a vacuum cleaner while it's on. "So intense!" wrote one person who tried it. "My piss got sucked in perfectly."

But most men seem to prefer to urinate outside, sometimes attempting to knock leaves off trees, extinguish campfires, write their names in snow, and so on. Peeing outdoors even became the subject of an entire "Dear Abby" column.

Charlton Heston, of all people, wrote in to defend the practice, saying: "The fact remains that **all men pee outdoors.**" (Yeah, but do they pack a gun while doing it, as he probably does?)

Another letter came from a woman who spent thirteen years trying to stop her (allegedly) grown-up husband from peeing outdoors. She finally succeeded **by peeing outdoors herself.** He was shocked, and said he hadn't come there for the waters. She threatened to continue her inelegant behavior until he abandoned his.

ON THE LIGHTER SIDE

Actor Richard Burton, a former husband of Elizabeth Taylor and a notorious drunk, was desperate to take a leak while playing *Henry V.* So, according to *The Dictionary of Disgusting Facts,* he turned his back on the audience and attempted to discreetly urinate through his chain-mail suit.

But the urine flowed down into the hot footlights and then boiled, letting off so much steam that the front rows of the theater had to be evacuated.

Penis Accidents

Electrolux sucks. There have been more than seventy reports in the medical literature of serious problems resulting from what has jokingly been called trying to get a **"cleaner, leaner wiener."** Injuries from misguided attempts to pump the pickle with a vacuum range from a fractured frankfurter to its entire loss—and even to the loss of the person who owns the penis.

Latent appliance fetishists, note: There is a fan in there.

Most penis accidents are caused by the choice of **weird objects for masturbation.** For example, one man foolishly jerked off in his machine shop by **holding his penis against the canvas drive belt** of some machinery.

As he approached orgasm, he leaned too close and his scrotum became caught, and was lost. Worse still, he closed the laceration using an available stapling gun, causing even more problems later when the staples became rusty.

Dumbbell: Sexual curiosity or testing (or improving) one's manhood may also be a cause of accidents. For example, some jerk-off decided to **see if his penis would fit inside a weight.** It did, but unfortunately it didn't come out.

The man had to enter the emergency room with a barbell weight stuck to his burrito. The two were ultimately disengaged only by draining the blood out of his organ, proof that ding-dongs should stay away from dumbbells.

Sex, ambulance style: One category of altered wangs involves accidents that most men think can't happen, since there are no bones inside a shlong. But **broken penises** are an occasional medical problem. They can be ruptured, just as balloons can be expanded until they burst.

So, if you're having sex (broken-dick accidents occur only during erections, sometimes because the man misses the woman's vagina) and hear a sharp cracking sound, it's probably not an earthquake.

And improve your aim next time.

There's a cock-and-ball story about actor **Michael Douglas,** who had a multimillion-dollar lawsuit filed against him by a golf caddy. **The caddy claimed his testicles were ruptured** and later removed because of a bad drive by Douglas. Talk about a slice into the wood!

Here's three "ouch" stories that could be subtitled "It won't be long now." One man had to be hospitalized after **his balls got trapped** between the slats of his lounge chair when he lay face-down in the nude to sunbathe.

There's a similarly horrible story of a man who went to his chiropractor, lay face-down on the table and his **genitals fell between the two parts of the table.** When the chiropractor adjusted the table along with the man's back . . .

And a young college boy being hazed at a fraternity received a **wedgie,** not that unusual, except this one resulted in a ruptured testicle that had to be surgically removed.

"The dog ate my testicles" may not be a believable excuse, but it happened to a British twenty-seven-year-old who almost died from blood loss after **his Rottweiler bit down on him** while they were playing. And to add insult to a literal injury, the dog then played with them for a while.

Although what was left of them was not in good enough shape to be reattached, he still considered the pup his best friend afterward. "You don't shoot your best friend just for biting your testicles off," he said.

Bizarre and reclusive multimillionaire **Howard Hughes** had a dog named Chang, who got into a fight with another dog. When Howard Hughes tried to separate them, the **aggressor dog somehow bit Hughes's balls;** he required several stitches in his penis afterward.

A Scotsman's son dropped a toy into his father's bathtub while he was bathing, and the toy floated over to him, grabbed his dong, and wouldn't let go.

The father had to enter a hospital emergency room with a **wind-up turtle toy attached to his own toy.** (Moral: Stick with rubber ducks in the bathtub!)

ON THE LIGHTER SIDE

What are five problems about being a penis?

1. You're bald.

2. You have a hole in your head.

3. Your next-door neighbors are nuts.

4. The neighbor behind you is an asshole.

5. And after you get excited, you throw up on yourself and pass out.

Penis, Changing Size and Shape

Erection set. Some men spend over $5,000 for an operation that **adds only an inch to an inch and a half to an erect penis,** hardly enough to allow the person to change his name to Hugh G. Rection.

But at least one tribe in Uganda has found a free method to elongate the dork. They keep a weight on the end of it. The method is so successful that some of the men are said to have to **tie a knot in their penises when they get too long.** (Well, that's what it said in a fun book called *Facts and Phalluses.*)

Dream on: A fifty-two-year-old Turkish man tried to persuade doctors to **replace his penis with a donkey dick,** which he had cut from an unwilling ass. The story came to light because his son shot him to stop this nonsense, which, incidentally, it didn't. At last report, the ass was still plotting to find another ass.

Nearby, in Turkey, a leading Italian plastic surgeon asked health officials for permission to **transplant a penis from one body, dead or alive, to another.** The doctor said it was easier to transplant another person's penis to the patient than reattach his original one.

By the way, here's the whole story on **how they turn a penis into a vagina.** The contents of the penis are removed but the skin is kept, and then inverted into a surgically created opening. That way, the "woman" still has sensitivity in that region.

Organ grinders: *Facts and Phalluses* reveals that some Australian aborigines **slit the penis through to the urethra and flatten it out like**

a pancake. Other disgusting deformations of the dong have been done for a variety of different reasons. For example:

- **Birth control.** Some primitive tribes **cut the urethra** so that the semen can't make it to the tip.

- **Self-control.** Some of the ancient Greek athletes supposedly **tied their foreskins over the tops of their pricks** to prevent themselves from doing horizontal exercises and adversely affecting their athletic performance.

- **Decorum.** During proper Victorian days, some men wore **rings in their penises** so that their pricks wouldn't stick out when they wore the tight pants of the day. That way, women presumably wouldn't be offended by learning that men had penises.

A popular ring, the **Prince Albert ring,** was named after the most famous person known to wear it. (Queen Victoria's husband, that is, not Prince Grace's son, although who knows?)

This ring has become popular once again. Interest in it has risen not because of a resurgence of false modesty, but because it supposedly makes sex more pleasurable for both partners.

Two current examples of mild penile "tampering" include a craze among crazed women who go to male strip clubs. There, they make bets with each other as to **who can stretch the dancer's penis the longest—and who can get it into a pint of beer the fastest.**

ON THE LIGHTER SIDE

Some men go to any lengths to get a bigger penis, like the ones who mailed a company $25 in response to an ad promising to send them a **penis enlarger.**

They were sent a magnifying glass.

(For more on penis size, see also "Penises, Famous People's.")

Penises, Famous People's

Men generally want big penises, but many women find them disgusting. Women who want to know the truth about some stars should check out the "anti-FAQ" of the newsgroup alt.showbiz.gossip, which has some tidbits about **the size of celebrities at full mast,** including some direct quotes from those who claim to know. For example:

- ☻ **Don Johnson** was said to be "as big around as a beer can."
- ☻ **Ava Gardner** said of Frank Sinatra, "He only weighs 120, but 100 pounds is cock."
- ☻ **Errol Flynn** entertained Hollywood partygoers by playing "You Are My Sunshine" on the piano, using only his wingding.
- ☻ **Truman Capote** described famed playboy **Porfirio Rubirosa's** (Porfirio was once married to Doris Duke) as "an 11-inch café-au-lait as thick as your wrist."

Other well-endowed celebrities, according to *Penis Size and Enlargement* by Gary Griffin, include

Patrick Stewart (said to be the biggest)	**Matt Dillon**
Peter Lawford	**Woody Harrelson**
Charles Bronson	**Tommy Lee Jones**
Alec Baldwin	**Lyle Lovett**
David Letterman	**Jason Patric**
Jason Priestly	**Robert Redford**
James Caan	**Arnold Schwarzenegger**
Jim Carrey	**Jimmy Smits**
Dick Cavett	**Keifer Sutherland**
	Bruce Willis

When **Montgomery Clift** (*Suddenly Last Summer, A Place in the Sun,* etc.) died, his autopsy was performed by the Chief Medical Examiner of New York. The doctor's wife, a famous psychiatrist, was said to have discussed Monty's dick at dinner parties, telling people that she had seen it at the autopsy and that it was **small and shriveled.**

She also claimed that **she had flicked it,** which she would then proceed to demonstrate. Such revelations, when they hit the newspapers, did nothing for either doctor's career or reputation—but it did get them invited to a lot of dinner parties.

Apparently you don't have to be dead, just not moving, to have doctors laugh at the pistol you pack. The *New York Post* reported that one of the top plastic surgeons in Los Angeles had a lawsuit filed against him by four vengeful former employees. (The suit has since been dismissed.)

It was claimed in the lawsuit that he had **poked fun at the penises of Don Johnson and Michael Jackson, even supposedly exposing and "obscenely manipulat[ing Michael Jackson]'s penis** while thoroughly scrutinizing it."

Furthermore, on another occasion, while examining Michael Jackson's penis, the suit charged that he allegedly said something to the effect that Jackson had never used it!

As for **Don Johnson,** supposedly one of the most well-endowed men in Hollywood, while he was recovering from liposuction and not in a position to punch the doctor in the mouth, the doctor was accused of pointing to his exposed genitals and saying, **"Why would Melanie Griffith settle for that?"**

How bad is it for a doctor to do such things to his patient? A man named Steve posted the following to the Internet on this subject:

> Am I missing something here? So, you … are a patient of the plastic surgeon. While you're unconscious, he's literally peeling your face off your skull, stretching it, cutting off bits of it, stapling the rest back together in a welter of blood, doing things that would make a Nicaraguan death squad puke and faint, and you're upset that in the midst of all this he might have said something derogatory about your weewee?

Don't look down. The **smallest suspected royal penis** may have been the one belonging to the **Duke of Windsor**, who would probably have gladly given up his kingdom for another few inches. His teeny weeny wiener was said to be only about 2½ inches long—erect.

But if he couldn't get much of his micropenis up, that may have been OK for the divorced throne-wrecker, **Wallis Simpson,** because there were whispers for years that she was genetically born a man and couldn't get anything in. (And speaking of whispering, one wonders about Bill Gates and exactly what "Microsoft" is supposed to mean.)

The most famous detached member belonged to **Napoleon, whose penis was obtained** when the person who gave him the last rites took a little tip for himself for his work. The mummified member was then passed on to many people, displayed for the decadent for decades, and finally auctioned off at Christie's in the early '70s.

There, in the catalog, amid the jewelry and the tapestries and the art, it was demurely described as a "dried shriveled object measuring less than 1 inch." But there were no buyers that night. ("Not Tonight, Josephine," blurted the British tabloids.)

It was ultimately purchased by a urologist for $3,000; he still has it in his private collection, which he shows to a select few. ("Want to come up and see my . . . um.")

Hitler's sexual apparatus was immortalized in this little song:

> Hitler has only got one ball,
>
> Goering has two but they are small.
>
> Himmler has something sim-lar,
>
> And Goebbels has no balls at all.

There may have been some truth to this rumor about the **dictator's dick,** because a copy of an autopsy report states that the burned body identified as Hitler had only one testicle. (The same was true of **Napoleon.**)

When Walt Whitman's penis was examined after he died, it was concluded that he had probably been born a **eunuch.**

ON THE LIGHTER SIDE

Mark Wahlberg revealed in an interview that **Leonardo DiCaprio** was originally the one being considered for the lead role in *Boogie Nights*. But Wahlberg said he got the coveted part when he told the director **he had an inch on Leonardo**—and then proved it.

(See also "Penis, Changing Size and Shape.")

Penises, Unusual

There have been almost 100 reports in the medical literature of **men born with two penises**. Some guys wouldn't mind that at all, except that in some cases neither of the members works, and in others, additional, less desired appendages are often part of the package.

For example, at the turn of the twentieth century, a man who was a partial Siamese triplet **had two penises and a third leg**—plus two feet, belonging to his unborn twin, protruding from his body.

Lucky stiff: In the late 1800s, a man also **had two penises, which he could use independently.** He too had a third leg—developed enough to include ten webbed toes—but he was able to strap it to his thigh when he was walking so it wouldn't get in the way.

His two love pumps didn't seem to get in his way, either. They were slightly different sizes, and he generally preferred to use the slightly larger one for sex. Occasionally, he alternated one organ after another.

He was also said to have been able to use the two simultaneously, as to well as to urinate out of both organs at the same time—surely not as much fun as the first feat.

Two heads are better than one: Most extreme physical anomalies are quietly altered surgically around the time of birth these days. But a contemporary Peruvian announcer **born with two penises** refused to remove one, saying that both were a gift from God.

After he publicly announced his "gift," he became wildly popular, more likely a result of his endowment than of his religious convictions.

There have been medical reports of people with

- ◉ Two assholes
- ◉ Three testicles

- The **skin of their penis and testicles combined** (making erection painful)
- A **penis whose opening was halfway** along the shaft rather than at the end (not that uncommon)
- An **overly long foreskin,** which had to be tucked out of the way (again, not totally unknown)
- **A testicle in front of the asshole,** dangling from the back
- The **penis and balls transposed,** so that the scrotum sat on top and in front of the penis

Try explaining any of those situations at the gym!

ON THE LIGHTER SIDE

Are people born with more than one penis or two testicles chock-full-of-nuts?

Performances, Perverse

Now that's entertainment! Many people think shows are getting more and more disgusting, but the **Grand Guignol** in Paris pioneered grossout entertainment. **Eyeball gougings** were "perennially popular, animal eyes being especially useful for this purpose because they could be relied upon to bounce when hitting the floor," according to *The Straight Dope Tells All.*

At the Paris Hall, there were **disembowelings, self-mutilations, throat slashings, rapes, acid in the face, flesh ripped from the bone**—and worse—all promising a bloody good time for those who went there.

The show finally closed in 1962, so don't bother looking it up.

Fisticuffs: A showman in the last century who called himself "the Man with the Largest Mouth in America" repeatedly proved it by **swallowing his entire clenched fist.**

Kamakaze Freak Show: John Kamakaze, Scotland's self-styled Prince of Pain, set a stomach-churning record a few years ago when he spent fifteen minutes **suspended in midair by meat hooks** imbedded in his back. He said it didn't hurt at all. "The only thing that hurts is a blister on my foot from walking around too much yesterday," he said, according to Reuters.

"This Ain't Your Mama's Charity Benefit" features **HIV-positive performance artist** Bud Cockerham, suspended by hooks, while passersby slice and dice the willing victim with a razor. After that, he's wrapped in a bedsheet, and the bloodstained sheet is later displayed.

Brad Beyers, the Human Toolbox, can

- **Hammer a nail through his face** and hang a wooden board from it

- **Push an ice pick up his nostril**

- **Drill into his head with an electric drill:** "I know when I'm going too far because . . . I hear a crunching noise," he said as he demonstrated his sickening skills on the *Guinness World Records* TV show.

Wrestling or busting a gut involves two corpulent competitors trying to push each another out of a small ring using their bellies. A sport of sorts since Victorian times, it's making a comeback in the U.K., with stars like **Mad Maurice,** described as a man who could make his bellybutton sneer.

South Park has vomiting characters, anal probes, and discoursing dung, but the Brazilians and the Japanese seem to have the tasteless entertainment market cornered. On one Japanese TV show, **women in bikinis crush aluminum cans with their breasts.** On another, a young child was told his mother had just been shot to death. They wanted to see how many seconds would elapse until he started crying.

Some American movie goodies include **"Texas Chainsaw Massacre,"** which was voted the all-time gross-out movie by a magazine called *Charged.* Runners-up included:

- **"The Brain That Wouldn't Die"** —A surgeon keeps the decapitated head of his fiancée alive, while searching for a suitable body to attach it to.

- **"Night of the Living Dead"**—A group of seven people are hunted down and surrounded by flesh-eating zombies, while they're holed up in an abandoned house waiting for help.

- **"Tales of Terror"**—A man walls up his cheating wife; Peter Lorre splits the head of a cat with an axe, etc.

(Rent these video nasties for the guests who won't leave.)

Truth is often grosser than fiction. Most people think the frames in the **Zapruder film** of the Kennedy assassination where his brain gets blown away were pretty violent. Yet a major video outlet rated it only 5 out of 10 on a **video violence meter.** That was equal to the rating of that family holiday favorite, *The Ten Commandments*.

ON THE LIGHTER SIDE

Director John Waters, who helps people to get in touch with their inner gag reflex by showing such things as people eating dog shit, once said, **"If someone vomits watching one of my films,** it's like getting a standing ovation."

Semen and Female Fluids

There are discussions of joy juice on the Internet at *Bizarre* magazine's "Ask Bizarre" and websites with titles like **That Taste Below the Waist**. Indeed, the whole question of whether **foods can affect semen taste** suggests a variety of interesting at-home experiments. While you're rounding up subjects, here are some of the findings so far:

- **Wheat may increase the amount of semen** one produces.

- **Semen can be sweetened by drinking pineapple juice,** or by eating bananas or papayas.

- **Red meat can make semen taste more acidic.** (Semen is commonly said to naturally taste acidic or salty.)

- **Alcohol or coffee** may make semen more bitter.

- **Garlic** may give semen a bad taste.

- Semen taste may also be affected by **beer, curry, cigarettes, joints, asparagus, broccoli, vitamins, artichokes, ginger, chili, and celery.**

- Its taste may be altered by **diabetes or stress.**

- One woman described the taste—not the experience—of semen as like **"swallowing snot."**

- Others have reported that it tasted like **Clorox, rancid Elmer's glue, thick globby beer, Brie cheese, and Ajax.**

- One woman said she could tell if her boyfriend had just eaten **hamburgers and onions** at the local fast-food place.

- Another woman reported that it **tasted like tacos,** perhaps because, as she admitted, that's all her man ever ate.

A little Vaseline or gelatin with a little coconut milk for color and voilà, you've got "semen." One trickster suggested the following amusing practical joke. You obtain a copy of a **dirty men's magazine.** Then you smear some of this **fake semen** between the pages of the centerfold, close it, and leave it in on the floor in a men's room stall.

The man who later sits down there will doubtless pick it up—and be totally grossed out when he opens it.

Not just for breakfast any more: The taste and smell of women's **crotch juices** are touched on in many of the semen discussions. Conclusions vary. For example, one man said, **"It smells like fish,** but it doesn't have as much taste."

Here is what others had to say about the **smell of "joy juice":**

 Women who smoke have a stronger taste.

 The taste varies according to the time of the month.

 Some say the taste reminds them of **blood,** or that it's **salty and metallic.**

 Others have said that to them it smells/tastes like a combination of **citrus and MSG, soy sauce, light Kikkoman, an artichoke tuna salad,** and a **musty armpit.**

Taco Belle: One man (maybe the one who eats only tacos) insisted that women's juices, to him, tasted like "the combined flavors of **fried hamburger meat, cheese, corn shell, and El Paso taco sauce.** I'll always have some fond memories whenever I eat Mexican."

The dank continent, and more on vaginal juices: One African tribe in Uganda has a custom for its unmarried women called "kachapati," or **spraying the walls with female secretions.**

Use your imagination for this one.

ON THE LIGHTER SIDE

A takeoff on the advertising campaign in which famous people are photographed with milk on their upper lip with the slogan "Got Milk?" has pictures of:

- ⊚ **Richard Nixon,** with a white mustache and the phrase "Got Milk?"

- ⊚ **Ronald Reagan,** with the same white mustache and the same phrase: "Got Milk?"

- ⊚ Federal fellatrix **Monica Lewinsky,** with a white mustache and the phrase *"Not* Milk."

Sex, Death During

Sex brings joy and pleasure for most, but some sickos seek out bizarre forms of sexual activity that can lead to pain (which brings them pleasure), and even death, which probably doesn't do much for them afterward.

For example, occasionally people are into apotemnophilia, or the **desire to have a limb removed,** and that has proved fatal in at least one case. A seventy-five-year-old doctor in Mexico removed the healthy limb of an eighty-year-old pervert who had wanted to be an amputee all his life. Not only did this man get his wish—he also got gangrene.

After he died, it came out that the doctor's medical license had been revoked years earlier, after three of his patients almost died from sex-change operations he had performed in garages.

Extreme masochism can also lead to death. For example, a forty-year-old airline pilot decided to **pull himself in chains behind a Volkswagen,** naked, in a deserted parking lot with his car circling in first gear. The chains got tangled, and he got squeezed to death against his car.

In 1987, a twenty-two-year-old Peruvian woman died of an infection caused by a rusty padlock that had dug into her body. It was attached to a **chastity belt** her jealous husband locked her into while he was away on business trips. He had been late returning home from one of his trips and couldn't release her in time.

Fortunately, no one will be releasing him—from jail—for a while.

Some people, especially in the rural South, construct a sexual toy using the heart of a recently deceased cow and a simple electrical circuit. A young man in Knoxville, Tennessee, tried this, plugging this heart into the electricity in his house. He was left charred unrecognizably—with the **heart frozen to his penis,** and his house on fire.

❖

Other fatal electrical accidents involving the sexual organs include

- ◉ Jerks who have put their **genitals in a bowl of water with a live wire.**
- ◉ Idiots who have **wrapped their penises in tinfoil** with one end of a wire attached to it.
- ◉ Imbeciles who have stuck **teaspoons up their asses,** aluminum around their pokers, and wiring in their mouths.

ON THE LIGHTER SIDE?

Medical examiners sometimes ghoulishly refer to these deaths as those in which **people come and go at the same time.**

Sex, Fowl

Fowl ball: Bestial moments with a fowl (avisodomy) occur more frequently than one would think—or hope. Think nobody you've ever heard of would do something as disgusting as that?

Hustler publisher and first amendment champion Larry Flynt admitted that when he was a nine-year-old living in eastern Kentucky, he was told by older boys that a chicken was as good as a girl, so he tried one.

Afterward, when the chicken was "staggering, squawking, and bleeding," he feared that his grandmother would see the hen and know what had happened. So, according to his autobiography, *An Unseemly Man*, he caught it again, wrung its neck, and threw it in the creek.

He got billed for doing it with a duck. Yes, there's something called a **duck job.** A man inserts himself into a duck, after which the duck's head is cut off. As the duck flaps and kicks, and its sphincter spasms in its last moments of life, it is said to provide quite the penile manipulation.

Consensual foul play: Some have tried to feed their goose and get off at the same time. **Grains of barley are sprinkled over a woman's vulva** and a hungry goose pecks them off. (Some women get more enjoyment from this than from than the average pecker.)

Fowl court cases: One man stabbed his eighty-eight-year-old neighbor sixty-five times **for raping his favorite chicken.** Worse still, as far as he was concerned, the neighbor was doing it in front of her baby chicks. Is there no shame?

Another notorious case was tried in an Irish court in 1931: A man accused of **bestiality with a duck** was acquitted after his lawyer insisted that a duck was not a beast—another case that proves the judicial system is often for the birds.

Is a bird in the hand worse than a bird in the stomach? In a famous case, an English court at first charged a man with **sexual indecency against a pigeon.**

But they changed the charge when they found out what he did to the pigeon afterward. He was then fined ten pounds for taking the pigeon home and eating it. (After all, gentlemen are supposed to take their dates to dinner, not *as* dinner.)

ON THE LIGHTER SIDE

One would think that **sex with birds is for the birds,** but as mentioned, at least one famous mythological incident features Zeus in the form of a swan ravishing Leda. This inspired not only paintings, but a poem by William Butler Yeats.

These codgers seem to have an altogether unhealthy interest in all this, which recalls a limerick:

> *There was a young man from Saint Johns*
> *Who wanted to bugger some swans*
> *"You can't," said the porter.*
> *"Instead, take my daughter—*
> *The swans are reserved for the dons!"*

Sex, Kinky

A psychologist with the imposing and ugly name of Krafft-Ebing catalogued all sexual perversions, with any number of cumbersome names. But it seems as if those writing about sex in the past often made it dry and uninteresting so no one would read it.

Not any more. Two startling and very readable books in this area are G. L. Simons' *Encyclopedia of World Sexual Records,* and another jaw-dropper, Brenda Love's *Encyclopedia of Unusual Sexual Practices,* from which most of the following comes.

Barbie Doll obsession: One man who shaves, and then **swallows, the heads of Barbie dolls,** climaxing when they go down—and out. Even worse, he then boils the same head and starts all over again.

An X-ray showed six tiny heads in the man's stomach.

(This isn't what a man means when he asks for "a little head.")

Here's looking at you, kink: **Licking their partners' eyeballs** gets some people off, which may be what Christian Slater was referring to when he said he'd love to lick **Jack Nicholson's** eyeballs.

Ocuphilia is a potentially dangerous practice, by the way, since there's a small risk of someone transferring oral herpes this way.

Reek and ye shall find: Some people are **turned on by smelling or coming into contact with other people's foul-smelling objects, like jock straps, menstrual pads, feces,** or just plain underarms.

Napoleon, in a letter to **Josephine,** requested that she not bathe during the two weeks that would pass before they met again. This may seem odd until you remember that Napoleon and Josephine were French.

In extreme cases, smelling is not enough for satisfaction, and the person may want to **ingest the bodily fluids or body parts** as well. In one extreme case, a couple of hundred years ago, a woman went to her husband's grave, obtained what was left of his genitals, and ate them.

Then there's the story, widely circulated among sexual-perversion aficionados, about a woman with a **colostomy bag** who finds sores around the opening of the bag, where the cord is attached.

It turns out to be herpes lesions from her sexual partner. It also turns out that this story is an urban legend.

I want my mummy! Some people really want their dear old mummies. Er, not that kind. They engage in **mummification, or wrapping the entire partner,** except for the genitals. Saran Wrap, duct tape (ouch!), and bandages are among the favored wrappings.

When the "victim" is immobilized, with just a few critical areas exposed (penis, nose), the mummification bondage fetishist then has his or her way with them. (Boris Karloff never had it so good.)

It's a wrap: Other versions of this include **wrapping one's partner in toilet paper,** spraying them with water (or worse), and then licking the paper off.

Necrophiliacs are those who like to **make it with the dead.** According to *Necrophilia for Dummies*, an outrageous document that keeps disappearing as it is chased from website to website, **"porking the bone"** is performed by extreme necrophiliacs who get turned on by poking skeletons.

By the way, necrophilia isn't always a crime. Twenty years ago, in California, a pretty young girl **"eloped" with a corpse.** The dead man was in the hearse, waiting to be buried, when this young mortuary assistant took him up into the mountains, where she could do what she wanted with him, since he was hardly in a position to complain.

When she was caught, the only things she could be charged with were stealing a hearse and interfering with a burial. She received about a week in jail and a two-hundred-dollar fine.

Most laws prevent people from secretly taping in places like bathrooms, but the law skirts the issue of what can be filmed in public if the person's face isn't showing.

Using video cameras to look under women's skirts gives some a sexual thrill, and others a financial one, since they later sell these "upskirt" (and "downblouse") tapes.

In one case, a man used a miniature video camera in a low-hanging bag, with the lens up, to look under the skirts of women standing in line. That's not so uncommon—except that it happened at Disneyland.

Is nothing sacred any more? Or, as the old joke goes, is everyone fucking goofy?

A little less innocuous: Videotaping people's butts turns some on. Stories occasionally crop up in disreputable literature (like this) about **Toilet Peeping Toms, or men who videotape or watch people in outhouses.**

Usually they sit directly in the sewage, staring up, sometimes with a video camera. One **pooper peeper** covered himself with a blanket with a hole in it, and hid in the bowels of the outhouse, affording himself a smelly but good viewing spot.

But this bum wanted to see more than just bums. He also cut a hole in the wall *above* the toilet, so he could stand up and see both ends of the women he ogled. He did this for over ten years before he was caught in 1998.

Here are some other kinks:

- Piesexuals. Some people are **turned on by pie throwing,** or by getting a pie in the face.

- **Club Mud. Mud wrestling or arousal by engaging in or watching people rolling around in mud.**

- **Felching is sucking semen out of the vagina or anus.** It's sometimes done with a straw, and it's always done with an open mind.

- **Queening.** The dominant female uses a man's head as her throne.

- **Genital isolation,** or restraining a "slave" against a wall with his **sex organs poking through a hole** and locked in place, or some sordid variation of this practice.

- **Some are turned on by people with scars, clubfeet,** and other handicaps, especially people with amputated limbs, or women with one or both breasts removed.

- The Trobriand Islanders practiced *mitakuku*, or **biting off a lover's eyebrows and eyelashes** at the moment of climax. (This is not the origin of the promise "I'll keep an eye out for you.")

ON THE LIGHTER SIDE

Joan Rivers once jokingly complained that it was so long since she'd had sex, she couldn't remember **who tied who up.**

Sex, Kinky, Asian

For some, it's the land of the rising sun—for others, it's the land of the rising *scum*. For example, some Japanese men are into high school girls and what they wear, use, or drool. Collectors go after **used underpants from high school students**—and these can even be purchased in Japanese vending machines.

An even less comprehensible collectible is fresh **saliva, spit out by beautiful teenagers**. Supposedly, the spit is bottled (with pictures of the stunning young donor on the bottle), refrigerated, and dated to assure the pervert that the spittle is fresh.

(Note: Maybe you find spit disgusting, but some connect it with sex, including a group of women from the Choroti tribe, who spit in their partners' faces during sex.)

Even more repulsive, one company claims that it's soon going to start selling **female high school students' menstrual blood.** Used tampons from teenage girls are already sold—to be inserted, perhaps, by the same Japanese men who buy oversized schoolgirl dresses to wear.

A trick of some Japanese prostitutes who work from boats, selling sleaze by the seashore, is to lean over the sides of the boats and put their heads into the water until they're just about ready to drown. The men, entering the women from behind—and often entering *the* behind—then **enjoy the vaginal or rectal spasms as the women nearly drown.**

ON THE LIGHTER SIDE

Here's a different slant: There are special coffee shops in Japan that have mirrored tiles on the floor for men who want to **look up their waitresses' dresses.** (The waitresses help out by not wearing underwear.)

Sexual Asphyxia, or Ritual Masturbation

Hoisted by their own peter: Since compression of the neck can enhance the vividness of sexual images, some people experiment with **choking themselves while they're masturbating,** usually using restraints such as ropes. Unconsciousness can result, and since these people are unable to release their bonds to save themselves, they can die.

Think it's unlikely? It's estimated that as many as 500–1000 people in the U.S. and Canada are killed each year by sexual asphyxia, also sometimes called ritual masturbation.

When someone dies of sexual asphyxia, how do people know it's an accident and not suicide, or even foul play, since the person is often tied up? One way: these victims may die wearing fetishistic clothing (rubber or leather), or women's clothing, such as padded bras, and even sanitary napkins. One man had attached a **metal appliance so he could pee like a woman.**

Some compress their necks because they're curious about death and want to get as close to it as possible without dying. Actor **James Dean was fascinated with dying,** and often drew pictures of himself hanging by a noose from the ceiling. If the car crash hadn't killed him, sexual asphyxia might have.

Most sexual asphyxia cases are hushed up by people's families, who attribute death to other causes. But in London in the late 1700s, an obscure composer and musician **went to a prostitute and asked her to castrate him.** She refused, but she did agree to hang him.

When he accidentally died, she was arrested. The case caused a huge splash, since sexual asphyxia was unknown in those days.

Knot for everyone: An even more bizarre case that also received some publicity around the same time, and was uncovered by the same researcher, Knud Joergensen, concerned a reverend who worked in old Newgate Prison in London.

The reverend was impotent from VD, but when he saw that **people who were hanged often had an erection,** he decided to hang himself *slightly* so he could finally get a hard-on.

He went to a female prisoner, who had been sentenced to death for shoplifting, and offered to show her how painless it was to be hanged. The first time he hanged himself it worked, and he got the desired boner. But he pushed his luck and tried it with many women, and it eventually killed him.

ON THE LIGHTER SIDE

Insurance companies often refuse to pay off on sexual asphyxia deaths, wrongly claiming they're suicides. A top New York City trial attorney, Albert Podell, once represented a widow trying to collect double indemnity for accidental death from her deceased husband's insurance company, which argued that a sexual asphyxia death was a no-pay suicide.

He jokingly suggested that if someone was going to practice sexual asphyxia, before each incident they should write a note, saying they've only gone out for a (no) breath of fresh air and intend to come back real soon.

Shit, Assaults and Lawsuits

It's a bird, it's a plane, it's oh my God! There have been several instances when the friendly skies turned into the fecal skies, as green or blue icy chunks of **shit fell from airplane toilets onto houses below.** (Happily, no heads—yet.)

In 1992, one frozen shit block crashed through the roof into a family's living room. When they called the authorities, they were told to store the waste in their freezer until someone could come and pick it up.

A cause of turbulence is those who shit *in* the airplane itself. In 1996, a previously respectable businessman became so intoxicated on a flight that **he got up on top of the first-class serving cart and chucked a turd right on it.** Not quite finished, he then wiped himself with the first-class linens. Later, he had to hire one of New York's most expensive lawyers to defend him. (It must have been when he saw his bill that he *really* shit.)

Plane disgusting: In a later incident of air rage, a man flying from Germany to Philadelphia also went berserk. He not only kicked the seat of a pregnant woman so hard that she almost had a miscarriage, but he **urinated in the aisle, and then into a condom.**

The **Mad Shitter,** as he came to be called, made his protests known in a crappy way. He defecated in books about the United Nations or gay issues, leaving them in aisles for horrified people to encounter throughout libraries in Ohio. It was three years before he was finally caught, taking a load off a lot of minds.

Oddly enough, he turned out to be the owner of a Catholic bookshop.

Here's muck in your eye: People who work in prisons frequently have to deal with inmates peeing, coming, or spitting on the food. Or worse.

Some prisoners throw a **"correctional cocktail," a mixture of feces and urine,** at the correction officers. (In the age of AIDS, this can be dangerous as well as disgusting to the recipient.)

In *God of the Rodeo*, the author described a prisoner who lined his toilet with paper, then "mashed and stirred the stool in a cup of water" before dousing his favorite guards. This was also called "shitting them down."

Wrestlers are another group known for their earthy ways. Indeed, some of those extremely corpulent sumo wrestlers have their apprentices wipe their asses because they can't reach them.

Another way some wrestlers live up to their image as unrefined (besides becoming governors): They "welcome" a new wrestler in their midst by **shitting in the new wrestler's gym bag.**

A story is told of a new wrestler who didn't like this game. So when he found a little present in his gym bag, he pulled out a nugget, smeared it under his armpits, put the perpetrator in a headlock, and just held him there for a while.

He let the man go in time for him to vomit.

Don't cry over spilt piss: Another "joke," revealed by a man who claims that he's done it, is to take some dog poo in the winter and place **a few frozen bits of turd in the air intake of someone's car.**

After a few miles, when the turds soften, the smell can drive people crazy, especially since they don't know where it's coming from. (A similar prank is to smear limburger cheese on their radiators.)

Teachers sometimes have to endure a lot of crap from students. Therefore, no one doubted a teacher in California when she said four of **her students had thrown *real* crap on her.**

She became quite the hit on national talk shows, reveling in the story of the vicious quartet who'd thrown buckets of feces and urine on her. She even passed a lie detector test, although knowledgeable people know that those too are crap.

Her story was questioned only when it came out that the feces were on the *insides* of her clothes. It turned out that she had soiled herself and blamed it on her students.

Here she craps . . . Miss America? One of the most famous people suspected to have used feces against a rival was a former Miss America. Shana Alexander, in her book *When She Was Bad*, told a long-whispered story about a famous former Miss America who lost her lover to another woman.

The beauty queen relentlessly harassed the man and his new girlfriend for months. On two occasions, the man received **a box of human excrement, once in an elegant Bonwit Teller box.**

Even worse, it was left outside his suite at the Carlyle Hotel.

When the boyfriend accused her of doing it, her response was a sarcastic, "Oh, sure."

So many deaths have been reported after people fall into various types of animal or human waste that it doesn't pay to describe any. But Reuters reported the particularly disturbing death of a teenager in a military-style Arizona boot camp after he was **forced to do push-ups over a pail of excrement** so that his head repeatedly dipped into the bucket.

You don't read about this in the crime reports in your local newspaper, but the police sometimes find feces left, er, behind at homes that have been burglarized. These appear to be a way for the thieves to say "Up yours," or, more accurately in these cases, "Up mine."

In one famous case several years ago, in Liverpool, England, a series of burglaries were committed by a gang of thieves. But one of them left something on the dressing table that convicted him. The **thief left a stool sample with his thumb print on it.**

ON THE LIGHTER SIDE

Ordure in the court! A Sri Lankan who was about to go into the witness box took out a bag of shit he had sneaked into his pocket, and threw it at a policeman.

Instead, it hit a—well, you get the drift. So did the reporters, who were thrilled that they could finally legitimately use the headline **"Shit Hits the Fan."**

Shit, Eating

As anyone who has a dog knows, some animals eat their own feces. Indeed, lab rats eat half of their own caca and it doesn't seem to harm them. It *can* harm humans, though—not as much if it's their own as if it's someone else's, since there's less danger of foreign infections from one's own body.

Still, it *isn't* safe, because parasites and hepatitis can be spread by oral contact with even a tiny amount of scat. So while **"Eat shit and die"** is generally not meant literally, illness among those practicing the repellent act of ingestion of substances expelled from the southern region of the body is a distinct possibility. (Assuming they aren't already "sick" to begin with.)

Fortunately, there is a great **revulsion against touching or eating shit** among all but the tiniest people. Very young children don't have this reaction to what comes out of their bodies, which they seem to view as natural.

Whether adults have this attitude may depend on whether they know what it is. In one study, they gave people two vials containing the same strong cheese and asked them to smell it.

If they were told afterward that the one they identified as cheese was really crap, their reaction to the cheese was one of total revulsion. (Did we really need an experiment to tell us this? And if they had done the experiment with Limburger cheese, would people be relieved to learn that it was really shit?)

Further proof of the relativity of what one finds disgusting can be found in a story told in *Dictionary of Disgusting Things*, an incredible (out-of-print) British book.

In the '50s, in Cambridge, England, a rich undergrad used to offer impecunious students a huge sum if they would **eat a plate of feces.** In one case, a man who really needed money got himself totally inebriated so that he was actually able to take a couple of mouthfuls.

He had just finished a spoonful when he found a hair on the plate—and immediately became ill.

Scat's entertainment: Around the same time, in America, at one Cornell University frat house, they would haze a pledge by bringing him over to a toilet, blindfolding him, and smearing something like strong aftershave lotion under his nose to desensitize his sense of smell.

Unbeknownst to him, earlier, they had put a piece of peeled banana and some toilet paper into the bowl. They made the pledge **take it out and eat the "shit."** (And who says colleges don't prepare students for real life?)

Here are two instances of people eating shit without realizing it:

- ◉ Tourists in places like Afghanistan have been sold sugar-coated cakes that were really **sugar-coated goat dung.**

- ◉ The following story could have been a slander spread by clerics in revenge for Voltaire's views of religion, but it was widely said that as he was dying, he panicked on his deathbed. Instead of using his chamberpot, he reached into it and ate the contents. (No, the philosopher's dying words were not **"I am, therefore I shit."**)

Love stinks: Some people eat shit because they enjoy it. This is most often done *à deux*, with a sexual component. Sometimes, though, the person simply **eats the feces of someone they admired.** A popular, albeit disgusting, compliment paid to pretty women in the Ozarks is, "I'd eat a mile of her shit just to see where it came from."

A detailed and absolutely disgusting document floats around the Internet periodically, telling its readers **how to "farm."** That is, how to go into a men's room, stop up the toilet, and obtain the feces of an attractive man who has just dumped in the john.

ON THE LIGHTER SIDE

Hook, line, and stinker! Italian researchers 100 years ago, trying to figure out how hookworms were passed on between their victims, made far too great a sacrifice for science. They deliberately **swallowed some of the infested feces** in order to understand the worm's transmission.

Brilliant! You eat worms and then end up with worms in your stomach. For this they had to eat shit?

Shit, Facts About

People have actually received grants to investigate whether people's feces weigh more in countries like India and Uganda than in the U.S. and England, and whether **those with high self-esteem produce heavier stools**. In the long run, not only do these studies waste taxpayer money, but they do nothing to help people get their shit together.

The origin of the feces: More practically, there are all kinds of articles on types and composition of feces, usually printed in gastrointestinal-type magazines.

Some contain facts almost everyone already knows: for instance, that eating more fiber produces more bulk. Others are more esoteric, like the **"sinkers versus floaters"** observation: If you eat more fat, your stool is more likely to float.

Joseph and the Amazing Technicolor Dreamturd: The **color of stools** has also been studied, and while this can have medical value, it can also be meaningless. For example, in one study, when mice were fed crayons, they produced shit that matched the colors of the crayons. (Think your hard-earned tax dollars are going up in shit?)

However, shit color in people can often tell you something about the health of the donor:

- **Yellowish turds** can indicate anemia.
- **Black tarry stools** can be symptomatic of gastrointestinal bleeding.
- **Bright red** can mean hemorrhoidal bleeding.
- Athletes on steroids have **white shit.**
- **Maroon feces** can come from bleeding in the lower intestinal tract.

Shit smell comes from a combination of noxious compounds, including indole and skatole (the ones most responsible for that familiar aroma), mercaptans (which skunks use in their spray), hydrogen sulfide (rotten-egg gas), and ammonia.

Some say the worst-smelling feces come from eating meat, and then vegetables; shit with the least smell comes from dairy products. Fat makes feces smell, well, like shit, and "a pound of pork chops followed by gin, a laxative, or an enema is a sure winner among scatological connoisseurs," someone volunteered in the alt.tasteless newsgroup, which didn't get that name for nothing.

If children take their first dump—called meconium—while their mothers are giving birth to them, it can cause a serious infection in the mother. (It can also cause fuzzy thinking in others, since midwives used to predict the future of the child by examining it.)

Sesame seeds, corn hulls, and tomato seeds often don't break down and may be seen practically intact when they come out the other end. There are many stories related to this **"second harvest."**

For example, someone who purchased human fertilizer for his plants ended up with some tomato plants he hadn't planned on, or specifically paid for either.

Those with strong stomachs read on: A recent newsreport in a respectable publication (unlike this one) reported that some people in famine-ravaged countries in Africa survive by picking through the excrement of their more fortunate countrymen, extracting the undigested corn kernels—and eating them.

Dogs who eat wild corn also sometimes later give their owners gifts of **large cornstalks** with actual ears of corn on them. (Yeah, but who'd want to eat those things?)

ON THE LIGHTER SIDE

Jay Leno once said, "Cops around the country are using a new weapon against criminals. It's called the Diarrhea Gun. Instead of shooting bullets, this gun produces sound waves that give criminals instant diarrhea. Now *there's* an episode of *Cops* you don't want to see."

Smegma, Sootikins, Fartleberries, and Dingleberries

Foul down below: **Smegma,** or **dick cheese,** is a cheesy substance produced around the penis, between the foreskin and glans, that provides lubrication for the foreskin to slide up and down.

It's a combination of decomposing skin cells and genital secretions, which can accumulate and become a foul-smelling, discolored, stinky mess.

It also sometimes hardens into ugly nodules called **smegmaliths.**

Sootikins are a kind of female smegma. It comes from not washing the vaginal area, which accumulates soot, dirt, sweat, and decomposing skin cells, along with residual vaginal and menstrual discharges. Ewww, gross!

Sootikins sometimes become so large and heavy that they drop off. In England, when poor women couldn't afford underwear, men were employed in London churches to sweep up the sootikins after services.

Ass you like it: Fartleberries, also called dingleberries, are at the opposite end from smegma and sootikins; little **pieces of excrement that cling to the hairs** immediately outside the asshole, between the ass cheeks.

They're more common among hairy people, and also among the homeless, or people unlikely or unable or unwilling to use toilet paper on a regular basis.

Odor in the court: **Fartleberries were indirectly responsible for solving a major crime.** Anal hairs were found in the cesspool under a farm that was secretly used as a hideout by those involved in the Great Train Robbery of 1963.

The hairs had become dislodged because when one of the crooks wiped himself, he had a rough time getting rid of his clinging fartle-berries. Samples of the anal hairs were matched with those belonging to all the gang members, and these were later produced as damning evidence in court.

ON THE LIGHTER SIDE

People likely to encounter fartleberries or dingleberries are those who practice anal-oral sex, and also nurses. They may have the foul task of having to cut the clinging or dangling objects away before surgery for problems like hemorrhoids can be performed.

So when a nurse complains about some asshole, he or she may not be referring to the patient.

Smell, Sweat, and Stink

Guess who *isn't* coming to dinner? Different societies have set different limits on what they would accept in the smell department of their members, but there's one group of people that everyone has to agree *stinks.*

According to *Nature Genetics,* some unfortunate people's bodies lack a particular enzyme that absorbs a smelly protein made by bacteria in the stomach. As a result of this deficiency, these people have **a horrible rotten-fish odor** that constantly seeps out in their sweat. There's little they can do about it, except wonder what it's like to have friends.

And speaking of smells and sex appeal, **Tom Cruise** admitted that when he was filming *The Outsiders* in the early 1980s, he **went weeks without bathing** in order to get into the angst of his character, and probably on the nerves of the other actors.

It's hard to sniff out why anyone would want to relive **disgusting smells,** but if you want to take a whiff of Henry VIII's sweaty feet, a severed head on a pole, or the River Thames awash in rubbish, you can buy a series of scratch-and-sniff books called *Smelly Old History.*

Merde! New studies show what your nose already knows. **The French don't bathe.** A recent survey published in the daily *Le Figaro* reported that the French wash less than other people do. They also wash less than they claim to.

King Louis XII of France **took only two baths in his life.** Long live the king—not! *Not* bathing was a sign of prestige. Of course people stank, but they covered it up with perfumes, oils, and spices.

French King Henri IV was described as "smelling like carrion." When his fiancée, Marie de Médicis, met her intended bridegroom, she swooned—not because of his appearance but because of his smell.

The sweat that oozes from your pores is actually **a weak version of piss,** made up of the same components as urine: water, salts, and urea. It also contains a chemical that is the same as wasp poison, and another chemical that is similar to what skunks spray.

ON THE LIGHTER SIDE

George Burns once said that when you're going out, you should "be sure to wear a good cologne, a nice aftershave lotion, and a strong underarm deodorant. And don't forget to wear some clothes too."

Snakes, Eating or Biting You

Some people think everything about snakes is disgusting, **especially being eaten by a snake.** When this happens (rarely), the snake covers its victims with saliva to make it easier for them to go down, swallows them head first until they're completely inside, and then digests everything, including the bones.

But digestion may be slow. One fourteen-year-old Indonesian boy who was swallowed by a reticulated python was still recognizable in the snake's stomach when the snake was killed and cut open two days later. He was found with his legs crossed, his left hand wedged between his legs, and his right arm bent behind his head.

Put yourself in that position as you think of what this poor boy went through, being slowly forced head first down a python's throat, drowning in the snake's saliva, and unable to move your arms, which are stuck helplessly by your sides as the snake's mouth grips you.

The U.S. government issued a policy statement for Peace Corps workers telling them **what to do if attacked by an anaconda:**

- Don't try to run away, because it's faster than you are.
- Lie on the ground totally quietly while the snake nudges you and climbs on you.
- Try to remain calm (sure!) while the snake swallows your feet and your ankles, and then sucks your legs into its body.
- And then, when the snake's mouth reaches your knees, quickly take out your knife, cut its mouth open, and sever its head. (But what if you don't have a knife?)

Of course, you're more likely to be bitten by a snake than eaten by one, and that's no fun either. If you get a serious snakebite and you can't treat it in time, **your limb may swell until it splits open.**

There's lots of fascinating information about snakes in *277 Secrets Your Snake Wants You to Know.* (That's where most of the info in this section comes from.) What does this book say is the worst place to get bitten (or squeezed) by a snake? (Actually, *any* place, especially if it's *your* place.)

Yes, of course *there*, as one man learned in 1993 in a Malaysian bathroom when he was **bitten on the testicles by a python.** (He also learned not to use public bathrooms in Malaysia.)

But experts say the next worst spot to be **bitten is on the eyeball.** And you don't want a snake *spitting* in your eye, either. Certain species of cobra, when threatened, if they can't get their fangs into you, will spit venom at you just as soon as look at you.

In fact, they'll spit venom *while* they're looking at you, from as far as seven feet away, with incredible accuracy. A spit in the eye can lead to painful burning and conjunctivitis, and if you rub your excruciatingly painful eyes, the venom can enter your bloodstream and you can be permanently blinded.

Here's spitting at you, kid.

The worst place for a snake to constrict you is around your diaphragm. That's where it's likely to happen, too, because snakes that are wont to do that sort of thing aren't interested in wrapping themselves around your arm to take a blood pressure reading.

Once the snake is around your chest, it will tighten each time you inhale. And if you struggle, well, the snake just wraps tighter. Once it senses no heartbeat, **the snake will begin to swallow you.** Whole. Incredibly, snakes rarely break any bones when they do this—not that it'll do you much good.

If you think what a snake can do to *you* is bad, though, think of what people all over the world do to snakes.

- Because it is believed that snakeskin is softer if it comes from a live animal, they're often **skinned alive,** then left to die in the hot sun for hours while someone goes off and stitches their skin into an oversized, overpriced handbag.

- **Their heads are put on meathooks and they're disembow-eled,** and then served to diners who can't tell the difference between snake and chicken anyway.

- People hate snakes so much that if they **run over them,** they may stop and run over them backwards to make sure they're gone. (What's that in back of you, singing "I ain't got no body . . . .")

- **People decapitate snakes,** leaving them alive, their eyes able to follow movement, their tongues still able to flick, and what little movement they have left taken up with writhing in agony from the massive and fatal damage to their tissues.

ON THE LIGHTER SIDE

The most popular name for a pet python is Monty—but a better one is **Julius Squeezer®.**

Snot and Nose-Picking

Most people think it's disgusting to swallow snot (snot for everyone), but you swallow a lot of it daily anyway; it just travels naturally down the back of your throat.

Picking your nose (or biting your nails) is a guaranteed way of picking up a few million germs—but your nose hairs are so thorough in picking up extraneous matter that the nose itself is actually one of the cleanest parts of the body.

Think no one will ever know it if you do it when you're alone? Scientists found that one kind of bacterium that is occasionally found in **human intestines** lives in nasal passages. It appears in the intestines only when one eats one's boogers.

A few years ago, there was an extensive scientific **survey of rhinotillexomania**—nose-picking to you—and 1,200 Wisconsinites agreed to answer a nose-picking questionnaire. ("Get your finger out of your nose and answer these questions.") Included among the survey's findings:

- 66.4 percent of pickers did it to relieve **discomfort or itchiness.**
- 2.1 percent did it for **enjoyment.** (That's all?)
- 65.1 percent used the **index finger.**
- Once removed, **the nasal debris was examined by most.**

Burger boogers: According to one judge, blowing one's nose into a police officer's hamburger may have been foul, but it wasn't a felony. The ruling came down after a disgruntled burger jockey showed his contempt for authority by **sneezing on a cop's burger.** All they could charge him with was a misdemeanor.

Nevertheless, don't try it. You may not be charged with aggravated assault, but the person you give the sandwich to may be.

It may be a man's life in the army, but the navy—man, what a life! One sailor complained that his fellow sailors **blew their noses into his coffee** just to see if he'd drink it anyway.

ON THE LIGHTER SIDE

You've heard the joke: You can pick your friends, you can pick your nose, but you can't pick your friend's nose. But most parents pick their children's noses. And some **Eskimos suck the snot out of their babies' noses** with their mouths. And a small (and suspect) survey showed that more than 10 percent of people had picked the noses of others, including their dogs. So just how disgusting it is depends on who it's done to and who is doing it.

Sodomy

Oral sex seems fairly harmless to most Americans. While you can't quite say "blow job" on TV, most comics, if they need to, manage to get the idea across fairly well, even in a country where until the '60s a TV couple's bedroom had to have two separate beds to avoid inspiring impure thoughts.

Oral sex, though, was no laughing matter (to teens it's actually a laughing, snickering, and hooting matter) to some lawmakers who included oral sex under sodomy laws.

Most people don't realize that voluntary oral sex may be treated (that is, punished) as severely as, say, involuntary anal sex, and there are people who have rotted in jail for enjoying consensual oral sex—in one classic case, as husband and wife.

And speaking of anal sex, everyone was self-righteously huffing and puffing about the cigar story in the Starr Report, after footnote Number 274 was revealed:

At one point, the President inserted a cigar into Ms. Lewinsky's vagina, then put the cigar in his mouth and said, "It tastes good."

But did he inhale afterward?

The most interesting tasteless activity in the report, though, was buried in a footnote ignored by most of the media. Footnote 237 claimed that when **Monica Lewinsky** had her period, she and the President of the United States, **Bill Clinton, "engaged in anal-oral contact** as well."

Did Starr really have to tell us about that rim shot?

During the wars that Russia fought with Turkey, the Russians had another reason to fear dying: It seems the Turks fucked the dying Russians in the ass so they could **enjoy their final anal spasms.**

Less than a hundred years ago, sex books advised that a wife might die and her husband could get cancer of the tongue if "he had the fatal habit" of **putting his mouth on her vagina.**

Even fifty years ago, not many women performed fellatio, so those who did became very popular. Popular enough, perhaps, to later become the wife of the President of the United States.

Kitty Kelley, in her deliciously gossipy book, *Nancy Reagan,* an unauthorized biography of President Reagan's wife, said of the First Lady that when she was a Hollywood starlet, before she married the future President, "she was renowned in Hollywood for **performing oral sex.**"

Although it's hard to picture Nancy Reagan, in her stiff hairdo and proper Adolfo suits, even bending down, nonetheless going down on somebody, one source told Kelley, "She not only slept around, she performed that act and she performed it not only in the evening but in offices."

The woman most people think of as history's greatest knockout, **Cleopatra,** was probably "homely as a toad," with bad breath to boot. So what was the reason for her legendary success with men?

Cleopatra gave great blow jobs. Her nickname, which has been translated as "Gaper," meant, roughly, "She who opens her mouth for 10,000 men." Well, not quite that many, but she was rumored to have **given head to 100 men** in just one night.

ON THE LIGHTER SIDE

Museum officials at Madame Tussaud's in Australia had to sew up the zipper on a wax statue of Bill Clinton because visitors kept sneaking into the exhibit and **pulling the President's zipper down.**

People also kept sneaking under the rope and getting on their knees to pose for photos so their friends could snap them appearing to service Clinton.

Spitting and Burping

Everybody in the drool! An average person produces 25,000 quarts of spit in a lifetime. That's enough to fill one to two swimming pools. Worse still, a baby will drool **thirty-eight gallons of spittle** in its first year of life. Maybe it would be better to put their diapers around their necks instead of their fannies.

Alan Alda may seem sexy now, but when he was a teenager and kissed his first girl, because of his braces she ended up with **saliva all over her face.** She waited until he wasn't looking so she could rub it off.

All it takes is a spew good men: In Tanzania, Africa, **the Masai people regard spitting as a show of good will.** Newborn babies are spat upon for good luck. Deals are often closed with a spit-soaked handshake.

Spit happens. Spit has been used to convict people. A suspected rapist running away spat on the street, thereby accidentally providing a DNA sample. The cop following him picked up the saliva with a tissue, and the DNA was matched to that of **semen the rapist left at the scene of the crime.**

The average person burps about fifteen times a day—generally a little more than they fart. Since belching is just another way of breaking wind, burps are sometimes called **mouth farts.**

Most gas comes from swallowed air (the rest from fermentation of undigested food), and since burps come from the same source, **the more you burp, the less you fart.**

Burps arise faster, though, because it takes at least thirty minutes for the gas to travel through your body and out your ass. And burps are more likely to smell like what you've eaten, unlike the noxious odor you get when the gas comes from the ass.

According to *Wireless Flash*, a burping-babies video features **thirty burping and crying babies** spitting up renditions of "Silent Night" and "Jingle Bells." The video was made by splicing together thousands of baby noises to form the melodies of the popular Christmas carols.

And you thought people had lost the Christmas spirit.

ON THE LIGHTER SIDE

Everyone knows what a saliva-laden French kiss is, but what's a **Belgian kiss?** Well, it's like a French kiss—but it's half phlegmish.

Tampons

According to the Museum of Menstruation, anecdotal evidence abounds that some animals seem more interested in females during certain times of the month. But the few times it's been studied, the theory hasn't been supported.

Sometimes it's examined by looking at numbers, for example in shark attacks. When those figures were studied, it turned out that **women divers with their period were attacked by sharks** *less* than men were. This may suggest that menstrual blood even has a repellent effect on some animals.

When bears were investigated, though, the researchers used more direct means. The U.S. Forest Service, in two disgusting experiments, gave bears a **choice of used tampons or garbage.**

The bears chose the garbage almost every time.

In the other study, they gave bears a choice of:

- **Used tampons**
- **Unused tampons**
- **Tampons soaked in nonmenstrual human blood**
- **A tampon containing rendered beef fat**

Again, the bears found the menstrual-blood-laden tampons to be, well, unbearable.

Here's a place where you don't want to have a spot of tea. In *Trainspotting*, a woman used a bloody tampon like a tea bag, put it into soup, and squeezed its contents with a fork.

A twenty-six-year-old man in England stuffed a tampon up each of his nostrils, to try to **stop his snoring.** When the tampons fell out, this rocket scientist used Scotch Tape to hold them in.

He fell asleep. Permanently.

ON THE LIGHTER SIDE

Empty tampon tubes are often used in homes as **hiding places** for money and other items. To do this, the author of *Offbeat Uses for Brand Name Products* suggests, "Take the Tampax [tube] out of the wrapper gently. Roll (or pack) the item up tightly. Put the Tampax [tube] back in the wrapper. No self-respecting crook, I guarantee it, will go looking in that box."

Toilet, How to Use in Space

It isn't easy to **take a dump when you can't sit down** because you're weightless. And even if you *can* sit down, what goes into your system doesn't necessarily come out of it so easily when you're weightless, as all astronauts have sadly learned.

In a weightless condition, in order to go to the bathroom, astronauts have to:

- Get the necessary part of their **pants off**
- Put on seat belts, foot stirrups, Velcro straps across their legs, and a bar over their thighs to keep themselves from **floating off the john**
- **Locate their assholes** so they can put the bag over the right place
- **Attach an airtight fecal collection bag to their behinds** and make sure they have a vacuum
- Get **what's inside to come out,** and detached from their bodies as well
- Peel the adhesive **bag off their buttocks**
- **Put the feces-filled bag back** in a special place

Not surprisingly, the whole process could take as long as forty-five minutes. And some days you think you've been on the john for a long time!

Former astronaut William R. Pogue wrote a book titled *How Do You Go to the Bathroom in Space?* It details some of the other problems astronauts have when they try to do what comes naturally in unnatural circumstances.

For example, the space toilets are often mounted on the wall—it makes no difference, since there is no up or down in space, but it does take some getting used to.

So does **crapping into a small hole.** "Occasionally fecal matter inadvertently floated free . . . and later drifted into view," wrote the astronaut.

He also said that no one would admit responsibility for it, and the floating turds later became, well, the butt of a lot of jokes.

Other flights have also had problems with evacuation—of the bowels, that is, not from the spacecraft. Being scared shitless might be an advantage up there, though, for on the first moon shot, one of the astronauts suffered terrible runs. **The diarrhea floated around the capsule,** turning it into a crapsule, as the squat stuck not only to the astronauts but to their clothes and the walls.

Usually astronauts had the opposite problem. To get the feces out, they often had to resort to the inelegant act of manual poking. To make it easier, they're given a bag with a rubber finger, to **pull the feces out of themselves.** Afterwards, the **feces are dried** by boiling off the liquids and returned to Earth for medical analysis.

NASA also had to make provisions for "outdoor" elimination, perhaps because they were concerned that some astronauts would take one look at the magnificent Earth down below and say, "Wow, that is so beautiful I could shit!"—and then do it.

So what happens to an astronaut if he has to **go to the bathroom while outside the capsule?** If nature calls while they're out there calling on nature, they do it right there, wearing special tight-fitting trunks underneath their spacesuits.

Urinating in space has always proved easier than defecating there, since astronauts can simply use a funnel-shaped device to collect urine. But to develop this seemingly simple contraption so it would also work for women was difficult, since they have problems urinating in space because of their recessed plumbing.

To develop a unisex toilet, **a group of women were first photographed urinating**—a job some perverts would die for—so they could be studied.

In the weightless state, there is also a constant danger of **urine drifting around.** During one flight, one of the urine collection bags burst, and the astronauts had to run around and try to grab hundreds of floating droplets.

Apparently they couldn't get them all, because one astronaut complained later that he felt like he was living for a week in a men's room.

One of the astronauts got a lot of publicity after his historic flight because he said he had seen what was perhaps a UFO, or at least a lot of mysterious unidentified lights around the aircraft.

Years later, the source of light was identified. It was believed to be crystallized **urine, which had been dumped from the spacecraft.** (Hey, don't throw that stuff out the window next time!)

And finally, a diaper soiled by astronaut Alan Shepard is in the British Museum.

ON THE LIGHTER SIDE

Just in case you're wondering, astronauts are not allowed **to eat beans or cabbage** before a flight.

Toilet Paper

François Rabelais, the respected sixteenth-century writer, stated that his favorite type of toilet wipe provided soft and heated cleaning for the anal area. What was this item that left him so flushed with excitement?

"Of all arse-wisps, bum-fodders, tail-napkins, bung-hole-cleaners and wipe-breeches, there is none in this world comparable to the **neck of a goose,** that is well downed, if you hold her head betwixt your legs," he wrote, according to Cecil Adams.

Other toilet paper types depended on where the person lived and what was readily available and disposable:

- Aristophanes wrote that the rich used **leeks** when they took a leak.

- Sea folks used **mussel shells.**

- Hawaiians used **coconut husks.**

- Medieval monks used **pottery shards.**

- In the seventeenth century, rich people in France used unspun **hemp.**

- The court of Louis XIV used **lace.**

- Colonial Americans preferred **corn husks**—two of them, in fact. The darker one was used to carry out the initial paperwork, and then they wiped themselves with light corn husks to see if they needed more cleaning. So put that in your corncob pipe and smoke it.

How to Shit in the Woods is a popular book that tells campers how to get rid of their wastes and how to build a latrine—and the pages can be used afterward as toilet paper!

One suggestion in the book, for rock climbers without access to a toilet, is to **"shit on a rock,"** using a spatula or a stone, to "frost" the side of the rock that receives optimum sun . . . as thinly as possible . . . Pretend you're frosting a cake." The ultraviolet rays from the sun will bake the "pathogens and dehydrate your leavings until wind carries off the final parched flakes."

Does the right hand know what the left hand is doing? A common method of wiping oneself in many parts of the world, such as India, is to **use the left hand as a substitute for toilet paper** and the right one for all other purposes.

We hope you'll never get a dyslexic Indian waiter who confuses right from left.

Islamic tradition also suggests the use of stones and earth, so pious men carry **dirt in their turbans.** Now you know what's on some of their minds.

ON THE LIGHTER SIDE

Bottoms up—especially if the bottom is cleaned with a book or catalog. The world's most famous toilet paper was once the **Sears Roebuck catalog,** a perfect blending of toilet reading and toilet tissue. But its use for that purpose died out when color printing came in; it coated the paper and made it nonabsorbent.

After that, one picture was no longer worth a thousand turds.

Toilets

Almost three billion people in this world are toiletless, often forced to resort to **open-air defecation.** Most of these people are in Third World countries, but outhouses are still used by 10 percent of all Americans.

As primitive as they are, they're still an improvement over other more widely used disposal methods. For example, **chamberpots** were once popular throughout Europe, and people would empty them out the window, screaming first to warn passersby. Most of the time.

For centuries, castles used **poop chutes as toilets,** until the owners realized that when they came under attack, the poop chute was a perfect entrance into the castle. Perfect—except for the poor soldier who had to go in that way.

The most famous person to die on the john was **Elvis Presley.** The official cause of death was said to be heart failure brought on by straining while attempting to evacuate. But the ten drugs in his system probably played a greater role than his constipation that night.

By the way, Elvis Presley and **Judy Garland** may have been the most famous people to die on the john, but the most famous person to be *born* in a bathroom was **Winston Churchill.**

Sore loser: A Jackson, Mississippi, gambler sued for $50,000 after **he got stuck to a toilet seat** smeared with Krazy Glue. The man had to be pried off, and then underwent the humiliation of having to walk through crowds of gamblers, waddling like a duck, with a towel covering his ass.

The man probably thought they were talking about him if he heard the term "crap out" as he passed a dice table.

ON THE LIGHTER SIDE

An old childhood rhyme goes as follows:

In days of old when knights were bold
And toilets weren't invented
They left their load upon the road
And walked off so contented.

Toilets, Cleanliness of

Can you catch anything from a toilet seat? It depends on who is sitting on it when you sit down there.

As if there weren't enough things to terrify the germ-phobic, studies have shown that many toilets **spray their bacteria up** when people think they're flushing them down. Even if you're not facing it, each flush releases hundreds of thousands of contaminated droplets, which often settle on your toothbrush, since most people leave those out in the open in their bathrooms.

Would closing the toilet seat lid before you flush help? No, because you'd still have to open it eventually, and then a cloud (which, fortunately, you can't see) containing these water particles would still burst out.

Here are a few findings about public bathrooms:

- ⊚ **Women's toilets have been found to contain more germs than men's** bathrooms, possible because children use them. (Or because a man did the research.)

- ⊚ **The middle stall is usually the dirtiest,** since people are most likely to use it.

- ⊚ The first stall is usually the **cleanest.**

According to *The Hypochondriac's Handbook,* **the dirtiest places** in a public bathroom are:

- ⊚ The sanitary napkin dispenser.

- ⊚ The floor around the toilet.

- ⊚ The sink.

- ⊚ The toilet seat.

- ⊚ The flush handle. (Especially since some people use their shoes to flush toilets and God knows what they've been stepping on.)

Badge of dishonor: To make sure employees wash their hands after leaving the bathroom, an Atlantic City hotel is asking them to wear badges with **electronic sensors.** If an employee doesn't spend at least fifteen seconds at the sink, the badge blinks.

If that seems a long time to wash, one doctor says the only way to get really clean is to wash your hands long enough to sing an entire rendition of "Twinkle, Twinkle, Little Star." (This is how obsessive-compulsives are created.)

A company once manufactured what looked like regular soap, but when people washed their hands with it, it turned their hands black. It was not a commercial success, probably because people preferred to be **slobs who didn't wash,** rather than clean freaks who had to explain to people why they had black dye on their hands.

In Singapore, they use cameras to make sure men wash their hands. In addition, elevators are equipped with cameras to catch anyone who might **pee in the elevator.** Considering that an American graffiti artist was flogged for putting paint where he shouldn't, God knows what they do to people who put *pee* where they shouldn't.

A Dutch company found that it could keep urinals much cleaner if they **etched pictures of flies into them.** Men trying to drown the fly reduced spillage by 80 percent.

ON THE LIGHTER SIDE

Rita Rudner said that the trouble with **men and urinals** was that men weren't demanding enough. "If they hit something, they're happy," she said.

Toilets, Types Today

To appreciate how advanced America is, one need only use a typical American toilet—and the toilet paper. Toilets in most parts of the world, when they exist at all, are disgustingly primitive.

Indeed, in some places they ought to call them **feet-ces** because they're just holes in the floor, sometimes with black **painted footprints** for people to position themselves for a bowel movement.

The smell is always horrible, the position absurd, and since flies and other insects tend to circle the contents, one often has to contend with unwanted visitors in there as well.

Shelve it . . . most of the time. In many countries, people drop their **stool onto a dry shelf** and then have to flush repeatedly to wash it away. It stinks, and it wastes water, but it's popular in countries like Germany. Now you know where the *germ* in *German* comes from.

Similarly, a Netherlands-style toilet is just a tray on which you do your business. And then the **refuse from your nether lands** does a roller-coaster slide when flushed.

Have can, will travel. Entrepreneurial Chinese, facing a shortage of public toilets, mount **potties on their tricycles,** offering a quick pit stop to those who have to go. (Hey, don't pooh-pooh it.)

There is an "intelligent toilet," used by the CIA which runs chemical tests on the contents of **foreign dignitaries' poop** to see if they have any ailments. As advanced as it is, they still have to station some poor schnook in the men's room to note which toilet the unsuspecting world leader uses.

It always seemed odd that Queen Elizabeth traveled with her own toilet, but now you know.

If you lived in Japan, you could buy a gadget called a Sound Princess that **makes a nice sound** so no one will hear the earthy ones you're really making while you're on the john.

ON THE LIGHTER SIDE

For the more gamy, there is a catalog that offers **Potty Golf,** a version of miniature golf to be played on the can. But what constitutes a hole in one?

THAT'S DISGUSTING

Urine, Drinking

I. P. Freely: Urine is actually quite clean—96 percent of it is water anyway—and there are no bacteria in it until it's out of your body. But although it's sterile, drinking it may carry a risk of **transmission of the HIV virus,** so it may therefore not be safe to drink someone else's urine.

Some also believe that drinking urine could strain your kidneys, since urine contains salts that your body is trying to get rid of. They suggest that if you're going to drink urine, you also drink lots of water as well. But if you're going to drink lots of water, why bother drinking urine?

Still, urine is a currently considered **a power drink** that's free and has been recommended by several sources:

- **Mahatma Gandhi,** who drank it regularly.

- Euro-peeins and English folks like the actress **Sarah Miles,** who helped make it popular.

- **Elvis Presley's mother** used to pee into a jar, and then put the pee in her beer with an eyedropper, believing it would confer health benefits on her, even if it wasn't all shook up.

- **Pat Boone** admitted on *The Daily Show* that he had tried it.

- *Newsweek* magazine ran a story about urine drinking.

- Environmental advocates occasionally publicly endorse it, advocating it as the **ultimate in recycling.**

- **Kevin Costner** drank it in *Waterworld,* whose title had nothing to do with that part of the movie.

- The leak(er) shall inherit the earth: The Bible says in Proverbs 5:15, **"Drink waters out of thine own cistern."** (It could have been worse. It could have said, "Drink water out of thine own *sister.*")

Don't say cheese: Occasionally other stories of historical urine drinking pop up. For example, a man in Germany was tried years ago for putting the **urine of young girls into cheese** to improve its taste.

ON THE LIGHTER SIDE

Gee whiz. Is there a doctor in the outhouse? At an **Auto-Urine Therapy conference** in India in the late 1990s, 600 delegates from seventeen nations discussed the medical benefits of drinking their own urine.

Probably a nice bunch of people there, but would you really want to go to their cocktail parties?

Urine, Facts About

Some people are totally fascinated with the useless fact that **their piss smells different after they eat asparagus.** Indeed, one pundit suggested that it's just a matter of time until someone produces a cartoon **Asparagusman,** whose primary job it is to sniff out people who have just eaten that vegetable.

Technically, the asparagus doesn't make the urine smell, some people just have the fairly useless ability to pick it out. There have been at least three studies determining how many people have this claim to fame, as if it mattered.

Tens of thousands of words have been written on smell hypersensitivity—even Benjamin Franklin, who surely had better things to do, jokingly suggested that a drug be found that could make a fart smell like perfume.

But if you feel you must know more about asparagus and pee-smell, you're probably best off waiting for the cartoon.

Here's a wee bit more about piss. Actually, your urine is odorless until after it comes out of your body. What you smell then is ammonia—yep, the same stuff you clean with.

Asparagus isn't the only thing some people smell in urine. Drinking turpentine is said to make urine smell like a rose, so hundreds of years ago, **women would drink turpentine so their piss would smell sweet.**

One man claims that large quantities of onions, especially in curried rice, make his piss smell odd, but so far this claim has not been backed up by rigorous testing.

If you really want to know:

- Eating beets can **turn your urine red.**
- **Vitamin B₂** makes it bright yellow.

- ⊚ Certain blue dyes make it **blue-green.**
- ⊚ **L-dopa** makes it dark brown.
- ⊚ **Rhubarb** sometimes makes it brownish or pinkish.

What's really important, though, is not color but intensity. A good clue to health is the darkness of the urine hue. Experts say that you should **pee pale.** (In other words, if you're not getting enough water in your system, your urine will be darker.)

Adult **men usually pee in a narrower stream than women do** because sex and children can affect the women's tissues there. This unusual fact was used to test virginity centuries ago: If a woman peed like a man, she was thought to be a virgin. (Some idiots in those days also thought they could just *look* at urine and tell if the woman was intact.)

ON THE LIGHTER SIDE

Piercing the prick may also affect the stream, since it can cause spraying, **split-stream pissing,** and so on. Indeed, after piercing, some men have to cover the hole with their hand in order to urinate normally. God knows what anyone next to them in a men's room thinks they're doing.

Urine, Practical Jokes and Assaults

For some people, sticking their hands in water makes them have to pee. Years ago, a man used to wander around beaches in Southern France, looking for sleeping women.

He carried a glass of water with him, and when he found an attractive woman, half asleep, sunbathing, he supposedly put her hand into the glass of water and then **watched her pee.** Well, it's a good story, anyway.

Remember the story of **Sir Walter Raleigh** and how he gallantly threw his cape down so Queen Elizabeth could pass by?

There are two things the history book probably didn't tell you about that:

- ◎ First, it was probably **a puddle of urine,** not water;
- ◎ Second, what did he do with his cape afterward?

Moo goo pee pan: Last year, after a tenant in Long Island became suspicious that her landlord was entering her apartment when she was gone, she installed a video camera.

She got a clear picture of her landlord, a forty-one-year-old computer programmer, removing a cardboard container of leftover **Chinese food** from the fridge, peeing in it, and putting it back.

This happened on three occasions in 1998, during which time let's hope she ate out.

Toilet water—literally: A Zimbabwean man was convicted (and sentenced to only a month) for **selling perfume that was really his own urine.** Fortunately, most women realized when they opened the package at home that it didn't smell like perfume and discarded it.

But one woman, who filed the complaint, applied it, took one whiff, and realized that what was on her wrists was more like Channel #1 than Chanel #5.

A twelve-year-old boy **removed the water from his teacher's water bottle and peed in it.** Apparently the water didn't taste funny to her, because she drank 8 to 10 ounces of it without ill effects. She only learned the truth because the boy bragged to his friends about what he had done.

She later sued the school, claiming the incident permanently damaged her ability to pee, ah, teach.

Waldorf Hysteria: In a very strange incident at the Waldorf Astoria hotel in New York, a fifty-year-old New Jersey fashion consultant claimed a naked woman trying to enter her hotel room awakened her in the middle of the night.

Even odder, she said the woman (somehow) supposedly **urinated on her door** when she couldn't get in.

She sued the hotel—not for that, but for the *food poisoning* she claimed she got from the basket of fruit the hotel gave her to apologize for the alleged bizarre incident.

Moral of the story: Ignore people who piss at your door, and never eat free fruit.

A joke to play with urine is to **freeze a small amount of pee** in a shallow dish, take it out, and then slip the "pee puck" into the mail slot on someone's door, tossing it in as far away from the door as possible.

When the frozen urine melts, the person will find a mysterious puddle near the door, and forever wonder how in hell it got there when no one seems to have entered the house.

ON THE LIGHTER SIDE

The Anatomical Chart Company sells authentic urine specimen bottles to give as house gifts, so recipients **can serve their guests wine like urine.** (It could have been worse; they could have served Gallo.)

Urine, Uses for

To us, a piss is just a piss, but historically, urine has been used in many unusual ways. For example, urine has been incorporated into wedding ceremonies. At weddings in North Africa, for ceremonial purposes, **the bride's urine was sprinkled on the guests** after the wedding. (Perhaps as a symbol of the sort of treatment the groom should come to expect.)

"You may now piss the bride": Sometimes, even in "civilized" countries like England and Ireland, **the guests drink the bride's urine.**
   (See also "Urine, Drinking.")

Because of its antiseptic properties, urine was once used to **wash wounds on the battlefield.** Centuries ago, when someone's nose was cut off during a duel, the surgeon peed on it to clean it before it was stitched back on.

Urine has been used to make tweeds. According to *Almanac of the Gross,* Harris tweed is still made today in Scotland the way it was made for hundreds of years. From yarn dyed with lichen—that has been soaked in human urine.

Urine was used as an **eyewash**—recommended in the thirteenth century by Pope John XXI, no less! And one pharaoh claimed he got his eye cured with the urine of a woman—whom he later thanked by marrying.

A squirt a day keeps the dentist at bay: Long ago, **urine was often used as toothpaste.** It was believed that brushing one's teeth with urine would make the teeth whiter. It may have actually worked, too, because ammonia is a product of stale urine.

Urine has also been used as a mouthwash. Bad enough to swish it around in one's mouth, but it was said to be most effective if kept in the mouth for long periods of time.

Urine may also repel cats and dogs. (Not to mention brothers, sisters, boyfriends, girlfriends, and strangers.) In a bizarre letter to the editor of the *New England Medical Journal,* a doctor wrote that two of his patients who had applied urine around the edges of their gardens had successfully kept neighboring dogs and cats from entering them.

One man had poured sterile urine out of a vessel; the other had urinated every few steps until he had accomplished his goal. Not satisfied with merely freaking out his neighbors, he insisted on telling everyone about it.

A few other recorded uses for urine:

- **To get rid of acne.**
- **To wash linens.** The Romans used to do this.
- To **tan leather.**

ON THE LIGHTER SIDE

Uncivil war: Richard Zachs, in *History Laid Bare*, reveals that urine was distilled into nitre for gunpowder during the Civil War. It seems that Confederate wagons went down the streets so women could donate the pee from their chamberpots. This inspired an amusing poem by an Alabama soldier, part of which went as follows:

> *We thought the girls had work enough making shirts and kissing*
> *But you have put the pretty dears to patriotic pissing.*
> *. . . But 'tis an awful idea . . . gunpowdery and cranky,*
> *That when a lady lifts her skirts, she's killing off a Yankee!*

This inspired a retaliatory verse from a Northerner:

. . . And vice versa, what would make a Yankee soldier madder
Than dodging bullets fired from a pretty woman's bladder?
They say there was a subtle smell that lingered in the powder
And as the smoke grew thicker and the din of battle louder
There was found to this compound one serious objection
No soldier boy did sniff the stuff without having an erection!

Vaginas

Fly-catcher, manhole, love tunnel, divine scar, prick-pocket, fart-Daniel, mouth that cannot bite, oyster catcher, hairy ring, bearded lady, dog's mouth, cat's head cut open, black hole, and meat grinder—these are just a few of the colorful names given to the vagina.

Famed sex researchers Masters and Johnson say there may be as many as 20,000 women in America who were **born without a vagina.** (Beats "Sorry, I have a headache" as an excuse!)

At least one of these **women born without a vagina supposedly gave birth to a baby through her ass.** (Don't ask how she got pregnant in the first place.)

A twenty-year-old woman went to Johns Hopkins for some minor problem and was discovered to have a major problem: **two vaginas.**

Another woman had two uteruses: one opening into the vagina, the other into the anus. (So that's where Jerry Falwell comes from.)

Women occasionally have **unusually long clitorises,** sometimes even as long as a finger. There is a report in the medical literature of one case in which the stretched clitoris was so hard that it broke off.

Certain African tribes believe that **long labia** are beautiful labia, so they stretch them, tying them together with a string and hanging a rock at the end. This **Hottentot apron,** as it's called, may hang down as much as seven inches from the vagina. It can become so prominent (and uncomfortable) that a woman has to push it back into her snatch before she can walk comfortably.

❀

Several hundred years ago, when girls reached puberty, their families **put black ants into their vaginas** to make the labia and clitoris swell.

ON THE LIGHTER SIDE

Labial piercings have come back into fashion among a small group of people for whom tongue and nose holes are insufficient ritual adornment. So, one could say that in the '50s and the '60s, people got pinned, but today they're getting pierced.

Vaginas, Playing Tricks with

What can women do with their snatches? Yes, of course *that,* but some women can also do things with them that God never intended. For example, one woman could play **"Mary Had a Little Lamb" on a flute with her vagina.** According to *Stupid Sex,* one time when she did this, a fight broke out in the Calgary, Canada, audience that was listening to her when some man, for some reason, kept screaming that she should instead play "Over The Rainbow."

Some women have inserted as many as **seventy coins up their twats** and walked around without letting any of them fall out. (One man got kicked out of a bar after he first heated one of the coins with a Bic lighter.)

There was once a place called the "Half-Crown Chuck Office," open only to women who had **successfully stood on their heads, spread their legs, and had men chuck half crowns into their vaginas.**

Women have played "Tank Wars," **putting hand lotion into their vaginas and squirting it** at each other while crab-walking.

Women have **played billiards** of sorts. They sat against a wall and spread their legs, while men at the other side of the room would flick glass marbles into them. (One can only imagine the calls: "Bank shot off Jenny and into Christine's side pocket.")

Some women can **drink whiskey and smoke cigars** with their private parts.

Other favorite insertions during shows have included **walnuts and hazelnuts** (are these women *nuts?*), which were then shot into the audience.

ON THE LIGHTER SIDE

Blowing out a candle is a common trick, and it's not always a total turn-on. "The guys in the front row said you could feel the breeze and smell the anchovies," one man wrote after attending one of these less-than-dazzling performances.

Vomiting

Bulimia as a dieting method appears to be in vogue now. A paper reports that a new fad among teenagers is bulimia parties. While it's not quite like a bulimic bachelor party—where instead of a girl coming out of a cake, the cake comes out of the girl—it's said that some teenagers are having **scarf-and-barf parties**. They get together, binge on their favorite fattening foods, and then go to the bathroom and throw it all up.

Deliberately getting rid of food after ingesting it goes back a long way. Special areas called **vomitoriums,** in which people were encouraged to throw up after a meal, were popular in ancient times.

Barfing was not only accepted but expected after a banquet. It was a means of getting rid of the prodigious quantities of food and drink pigs gluttonously ingested at their bacchanalian gatherings, and it was believed to prevent hangovers the next day.

Devotees sometimes stuck feathers, such as those from peacocks, down their throats to stimulate their gag reflex. Indeed, practicing this led to the death of Emperor Claudius I, best known to PBS viewers from *I, Claudius.*

On New Year's Eve, 1998, **vomit vigilantes** (euphemistically called "Clean Teams") were dispatched throughout New York City's Grand Central Station. They were supposed to **thrust a throw-up bag** under the chin of anyone who seemed to be ready to throw up.

Last year, two Muslims went to Denny's and asked for their food to be prepared separately from the rest so they wouldn't have to touch pork. Afterward, they sued Denny's, saying the employees deliberately put ham and bacon in their food.

Jon Stewart, on the *Daily Show,* reported on this case, saying, "They claim their souls were poisoned and they had to **purge themselves by**

vomiting, two things that usually go unnoticed during Denny's breakfast hours."

If **your vomit looks like what you ate,** you just ate. If it's soupy, it's been in your stomach for a while. (Unless it's chicken à la king, which always looks like that.)

That **painful taste when you vomit** comes from hydrochloric acid, which is so strong it can go through stainless steel and eat through paint; a form of it is even used by bricklayers to clean mortar.

Many children can vomit at will, and some child psychologists say the best way to stop a child from doing this for attention is to make the child **eat it afterward.**

If you try to stop yourself from throwing up by closing your mouth, the **vomit will just come out your nose.**

Scary rides on amusement parks sometimes **turn vomit into a lethal weapon.** People puke and the vomit flies around, covering not only the bodies and faces of others on the ride, but sometimes the pukers' noses and mouths, preventing them from breathing. Centrifugal-force rides are especially risky.

People who are into **Roman showers are aroused by vomit.** It is said that some men of this type get their women drunk, then try to cause a gag reflex by sticking their penises down the women's throats.

ON THE LIGHTER SIDE

A sign in a church in England pointed out that the bowl in the back of the church that was marked **"For the Sick"** was "for monetary donations only."

Vomiting by Celebrities

Sticking one's finger down one's throat is generally a secret and solitary sin that rarely comes to light. And when it does, it becomes the object of horror—and jokes. **Weirdo in the Rye** and **Retcher in the Rye** are names the press began using famed reclusive author **J. D. Salinger** after Joyce Maynard revealed his bulimia in her book of memoirs, *At Home in the World.*

She said Salinger would eat pizza and other no-nos, and was so afraid of being poisoned by junk food that "he show[ed] me how to put my finger down my throat and make myself throw up."

He did this after telling her, "You can't let this junk sit around putrefying in your intestine." (No wonder he doesn't want anyone to know anything about him.)

Princess Di became the **Puking Princess** after she admitted publicly that she had indulged in bulimia for years, starting on her honeymoon with Prince Charles.

Joan Rivers, in her autobiography, *From Mothers to Daughters*, said, **"Bulimia was wonderful**. . . . How great it was to have all I wanted and throw up. It's heaven."

There have been lots of rumors about actress **Calista Flockhart,** including Internet posts such as the following after Calista appeared on a TV talk show:

Ewwwwww. . . . She twisted her bony, anorexic legs about her, talked like she was about to faint, and had the most grotesque teeth of a bulimic I've ever seen. The backs of teeth rot because of the bile from vomiting. She's got 'em. . . .

Actor **Nicolas Cage** (*Leaving Las Vegas, Raising Arizona, Moonstruck,* etc.) became so nervous when he kissed a young girl he had taken to the prom that he **threw up all over his shoes.** The limousine driver wouldn't let him back in the car after that, and he had to walk home.

Who will ever forget—certainly not the puker or the owner of the lap he threw up on—the diplomatic gaffe at an official dinner in 1992, when then-president of the United States **George Bush** vomited on his host?
So much for what he thought of the meal (or of his host).

Great moments in vomiting history: Other than Bush, the most famous vomiter historically was a man in the 1930s, known as the Great Waldo, who gained fame by swallowing objects and then regurgitating them.
The lowlight of his act was **swallowing a live mouse**—and then tossing his cookies, or rather the mouse.

A prominent Gulf War Syndrome activist, who claimed he had the symptoms and tried to get the government to investigate it, insisted that one of his symptoms was **glow-in-the dark vomit.**

A couple of years ago, an unidentified man in the audience at a Eugene, Oregon, city council meeting walked up to the controversial mayor and **threw up on his shoulder.** Everybody's a critic.

ON THE LIGHTER SIDE

An Australian comedian used to bring along a package of chopped mixed vegetable salad on his plane rides, and when no one was looking, quietly pour it into his airsickness bag.
If the plane hit any turbulence, **he would pretend throw up loudly.** Then, when he felt enough people were watching him, he would calmly start eating the contents of the bag.

Bibliography

Adams, Cecil. *Return of the Straight Dope*. New York: Ballantine Books, 1994.

——. *The Straight Dope Tells All*. New York: Ballantine Books, 1998.

Arnold, Nick. *Disgusting Digestion*. London: Scholastic Children's Books, 1998.

Bathroom Reader's Institute, The. *Uncle John's Fourth Bathroom Reader*. New York: St. Martin's Press, 1989.

Bogdan, Robert. *Freak Show: Presenting Human Oddities for Amusement and Profit*. Chicago: University of Chicago Press, 1988.

Booth, Dottie. *Nature Calls: The History, Lore, and Charm of Outhouses*. Berkeley, California: Ten Speed Press, 1998.

Branzei, Sylvia. *Grossology*. Reading, Massachusetts: Addison-Wesley, 1997.

——. *Grossology Begins at Home*. Reading, Massachusetts: Addison-Wesley, 1995.

Cassingham, Randy. *This Is True: Glow-in-Dark Plants Could Help Farmers*. Boulder, Colorado: Freelance Communications, 1997.

——. *This Is True: Pit Bulls Love You, Really*. Boulder, Colorado: Freelance Communications, 1998.

Cooper, Paulette. *277 Secrets Your Snake (and Lizard) Wants You to Know*. Berkeley, California: Ten Speed Press, 1999.

Cooper, Paulette, and Paul Noble. *277 Secrets Your Cat Wants You to Know*. Berkeley, California: Ten Speed Press, 1997.

——. *277 Secrets Your Dog Wants You to Know*. Berkeley, California: Ten Speed Press, 1999.

Dawson, Jim. *Who Cut the Cheese? A Cultural History of the Fart*. Berkeley, California: Ten Speed Press, 1999.

Elfman, Eric. *Almanac of the Gross, Disgusting, and Totally Repulsive: A Compendium of Fulsome Facts.* New York: Random House, 1994.

Flynt, Larry with Kenneth Ross. *An Unseemly Man: My Life as Pornographer, Pundit, and Social Outcast.* Los Angeles: Dove, 1996.

Fortean Times. *Strange Days #1 and #2: The Year in Weirdness.* New York: Cader Company, 1997.

Furze, Peter. *Tailwinds: The Lore and Language of Fizzles, Farts, and Toots.* London, England: Michael O'Mara Books Ltd., 1998.

Garbage, Greta. *That's Disgusting Too: The 200 Most Disgusting Sites on the Internet.* Berkeley, California: Ten Speed Press, 1999.

Gordon, David George. *The Compleat Cockroach: A Comprehensive Guide to the Most Despised (and Least Understood) Creature on Earth.* Berkeley, California: Ten Speed Press, 1996.

Griffin, Gary. *Penis Size and Enlargement: Facts, Fallacies and Proven Methods.* Aptos, California: Hourglass Book Publishing, 1999.

Guinness Publishing. *The Guinness Book of World Records, 1999.* London: Guinness Publishing, Ltd., 1998.

Kelley, Kitty. *Nancy Reagan.* New York: Simon & Schuster, 1991.

Love, Brenda. *Encyclopedia of Unusual Sex Practices.* Fort Lee, New Jersey: Barricade Books, 1992.

Lyon, Ron, and Jenny Paschall. *Beyond Belief!* New York: Ballantine Books, 1988.

Madigan, Carol Orsag, and Ann Elwood. *When They Were Kids.* New York: Random House, 1998.

Marston, Wendy. *The Hypochondriac's Handbook.* San Francisco: Chronicle Books, 1998.

Meyer, Kathleen. *How to Shit in the Woods.* Berkeley, California: Ten Speed Press, 1994.

Miller, Ian. *The Anatomy of Disgust.* Boston: Harvard University Press, 1998.

Moskow, Shirley. *Hunan Hand and Other Ailments: Letters to the New England Journal of Medicine.* Boston: Little, Brown and Company, 1987.

Parsons, Alexandra. *Facts and Phalluses: A Collection of Bizarre and Intriguing Truths, Legends, and Measurements.* New York: St. Martin's Press, 1989.

Petras, Kathryn and Ross. *Stupid Sex: The Most Idiotic and Embarrassing Intimate Encounters of All Time.* New York: Doubleday, 1998.

Pogue, William R. *How Do You Go to the Bathroom in Space?* New York: Tom Doherty Associates Books, 1991.

Rancier, Lance. *The Sex Chronicles: Strange But True Tales from Around the World.* Santa Monica, California: General Publishing Group, 1997.

Schwartz, Kit. *The Female Member: Being a Compendium of Facts, Figures, Foibles and Anecdotes about the Loving Organ.* New York: St. Martin's Press, 1988.

Shaw, Karl. *The Mammoth Book of Tasteless Lists.* New York: Carroll & Graf Publishers, Inc., 1998.

Simons, G. L. *Simons' Book of World Sexual Records.* New York: Bell Publishing Company, 1975.

Spignesi, Stephen J. *The Odd Index.* New York: Plume, 1994.

Spinrad, Paul. *The Re/Search Guide to Bodily Fluids.* New York: Re/Search Publications: 1994.

Stephens, Harold, and Albert Podell. *Who Needs a Road?* Miranda, California: Wolfenden, 1999.

Wallace, Irving, Amy Wallace, David Wallechinsky, and Sylvia Wallace. *The Intimate Sex Lives of Famous People.* New York: Dell, 1982.

Weingarten, Gene. *The Hypochondriac's Guide to Life and Death.* New York: Simon & Schuster, 1998.

Williams, Alan, and Maggie Noach. *The Dictionary of Disgusting Facts.* London, England: Future Publications, 1986.

Zacks, Richard. *An Underground Education.* New York: Doubleday, 1997.

——. *History Laid Bare: Love, Sex, and Perversity from the Ancient Etruscans to Warren G. Harding.* New York: HarperCollins, 1994.

References

Magazine

Bizarre Magazine
3330 Pacific Ave., Suite 404
Virginia Beach, VA 23451
(888) 428-6676

Internet Newsgroups

alt.tasteless

alt. folklore.urban

alt.showbiz.gossip

alt.fan.cecil-adams

alt.gossip.celebrities

Subscription News Services

Wireless Flash: www.flashnews.com for subscription information

This Is True: www.thisistrue.com (Note: the mailing list is free
but you can subscribe to a more complete service.
See www.thisistrue.com.upgrade.html.)

Internuts: Contact jschmitz@qis.net

Websites

www.msu.edu/user/eisthen/yeast

www.snopes.com

http://members.aol.com/JuliannaA/trivia.html

www.shocking.com/~despair/morbid.htm

www.urbanlegends.com

www.newsoftheweird.com

http://people.delphi.com/nlopez/afaq.htm (alt.showbiz.gossip antiFAQ)

www.officialdarwinawards.com/index.html

http://h.w.well.com/user/cynsa/newbutt.html (rectal foreign bodies)

www.Bizarremag.com

www.straightdope.com

www.Healthscout.com

www.mum.org (Museum of Menstruation)

www.wackynewz.com

www.farts.com

www.amnewsabuse.com

http://crash.ihug.co.nz/~ali/weird.htm (Ali's world of the Infinitely Weird but True (ish))

http://metalab.unc.edu/stay-free/10/semen.htm

www.thisistrue.com

www.flashnews.com

Additional Sources

Many sources are attributed directly in the text, but here are a few other sources for some of the sections.

Ass, Bizarre Objects Up and In: Darwin Awards; *Stupid Sex*

Bizarre Sex (all chapters): (Alt.tasteless) dictionary; *Dictionary of Disgusting Things; Encyclopedia of Unusual Sex Practices; Facts & Phalluses; History Laid Bare*; Internuts; *Men's Health*; Reuters; *Sex Chronicles; Simons' Book of World Sexual Records; Strange Days #2; Stupid Sex*; Wireless Flash.

Body Boogers and Disgusting Parts: *Disgusting Digestion; Grossology*; Straight Dope.

Body Parts of Famous People: alt.folklore.urban; *Facts and Phalluses; Goddess; Strange Days #1.*

Breasts: *Encyclopedia of Unusual Sex Practices; Sex Chronicles; Stupid Sex.*

Breath, Bad; Mouth and Teeth: Healthscout; Internuts.

Castration or Bobbitization: *Dictionary of Disgusting Things; Sex Chronicles; Simons' Book of World Sexual Records.*

Dismemberment: *Guinness Book of World Records; The New York Times*; Straight Dope.

Enemas and High Colonics: *How to Shit in the Woods; Hunan Hand; Playboy.*

Farts (all chapters): *British Medical Journal; The Re/Search Guide to Bodily Fluids; Scientific American*; Wireless Flash.

Freaks (all chapters): "A Cabinet of Medical Curiosities"; Ask Bizarre; *Freak Show; Guinness Book of World Records*; Morbid Fact du Jour; *The Straight Dope; Strange Days #2; Sunday Times* (Perth, Western Australia).

Kissing and Aphrodisiacs: *Simons' Book of World Sexual Records.*

Masturbation (all chapters): *Encyclopedia of Unusual Sex Practices; History Laid Bare; Simons' Book of Sexual Records.*

Menstruation: *History Laid Bare; The Re/Search Guide to Bodily Fluids; Sex Chronicles; Simons' Book of World Sexual Records.*

Museums, Records, and Collections, Tasteless: *Beyond Belief;* Reuters.

Penises (all chapters): AFP news service; *Encyclopedia of Unusual Sex Practices; The Intimate Sex Lives of Famous People; Men's Health; Pit Bulls Love You, Really;* Reuters; *Sex Chronicles; Simons' Book of World Sexual Records; Straight Dope; Stupid Sex; An Underground Education;* WackyNewz.

Performances, Perverse: *Playboy.*

Semen and Female Fluids: *Encyclopedia of Unusual Sex Practices; Playboy.*

Sex, Death During: Associated Press; *Dictionary of Disgusting Things;* Reuters; *Uncle John's Fourth Bathroom Reader.*

Sex, Kinky: Associated Press; Morbid Fact du Jour; *Stupid Sex; An Underground Education;* Wireless Flash.

Sexual Asphyxia, or Ritual Masturbation: Associated Press; *Dictionary of Disgusting Things;* Reuters; *Uncle John's Fourth Bathroom Reader.*

Shit (all chapters): *Almanac of the Gross, Disgusting, and Totally Repulsive;* alt.tasteless; Ask Bizarre; Associated Press; *Dictionary of Disgusting Things; The Hypochondriac's Guide to Life and Death; The Hypochondriac's Handbook;* Internuts; *The Re/Search Guide to Bodily Fluids;* Reuters; *Sex Chronicles;* Straight Dope; *Strange Days #1; Stupid Sex.*

Smegma, Sootikins, Fartleberries, and Dingleberries: *Dictionary of Disgusting Things.*

Smell, Sweat, and Stink: *USA Today.*

Snot and Nose-Picking: *Disgusting Digestion;* Internuts: *The Re/Search Guide to Bodily Fluids.*

Sodomy: *The Intimate Sex Lives of Famous People.*

Spitting and Burping: Associated Press; BBC; *Grossology.*

Toilets (all chapters): *Beyond Belief; Fort Worth Star-Telegram; Health; How to Shit in the Woods; The Hypochondriac's Handbook; Playboy; The Re/Search Guide to Bodily Fluids; Straight Dope* (Chicago Reader); *This Is True; Uncle John's Fourth Bathroom Reader; An Underground Education; Wall Street Journal.*

Urine (all chapters): *Almanac of the Gross, Disgusting, and Totally Repulsive; Dictionary of Disgusting Things; Do Men Have Nipples?; Folk Remedies That Really Work; Glow-in-the-Dark Plants Could Help Farmers (or This Is True); Hunan Hand;* Internuts; *The Re/Search Guide to Bodily Fluids; Strange Days #1; An Underground Education;* UPI.

Vaginas (all chapters): (Alt.tasteless) dictionary; *Encyclopedia of Unusual Sex Practices; The Female Member; Sex Chronicles; Simons' Book of World Sexual Records.*

Vomiting (all chapters): *Strange Days #1.*

Index

J

Jackson, Michael, 90
John XXI (pope), 153
Johnson, Don, 89, 90
Johnson, Lyndon, 6–7
Jones, Tommy Lee, 89
Josephine, 105
Joyce, James, 52

K

Kamakaze, John, 95
Kelley, Kitty, 131
Kellogg, John, 73
Kennedy, John F., 22, 97
Kidney stones, 78
Kissing, 68
Kosinski, Jerzy, 9
Krazy Glue
  in the eyes, 48
  on penises, 30
  on toilet seats, 141

L

Labia
  piercing, 157
  unusual, 156–57
Lawford, Peter, 89
Leigh, Vivian, 28
Leno, Jay, 120
Letterman, David, 89
Lewinsky, Monica, 100, 130
Liberace, 65
Lorre, Peter, 96
Louis XII, 123
Louis XIV, 4, 6, 139
Louis XVI, 36
Love apples, 69
Lovett, Lyle, 89

M

Mad Maurice, 96
Manson, Charles, 19
Masturbation, 70–74
  by animals, 17, 34, 71
  autofellatio, 71
  autopederasty, 71–72
  death during, 101–2
  "docking" technique, 71
  games, 70–71
  "pumping" technique, 4
  ritual, 110–11
  stopping, 73–74
  with strange objects/animals,
    16, 70, 72, 84
Matthews, Mark, 13
Maynard, Joyce, 163
Meconium, 119
de Médicis, Marie, 124
Menstruation, 75–76, 78, 109,
  134
Methane, Mr., 50
Miles, Sarah, 147
Mitchum, Robert, 54
Monkeys
  eating brains of, 77
  sex with, 16
Monroe, Marilyn, 23, 76
Moose Dropping Festival, 42
Mordrake, Edward, 64
Morris, Dick, 60
Mosquito museum, 78
Movies, gross-out, 96
Mud wrestling, 107
Mummification, 106
Museums, 78–79

S

Salinger, J. D., 163
Schwarzenegger, Arnold, 89
Scott, Sir Walter, 24
Semen
  choking to death on, 18
  fake, 99
  felching, 107
  taste of, 98
Serial killers, 78
Sex. *See also* Anal sex;
    Masturbation; Oral sex
  with animals, 8–17
  cats and, 34–35
  death during, 101–2
  in Japan, 109
  kinky, 105–9
Sexual asphyxia, 110–11
Sheep, sex with, 9
Shepard, Alan, 138
Shit
  aphrodisiacs and, 68–69
  assaults and lawsuits, 112–14
  bacteria and viruses in, 38
  color of, 118–19
  eating, 115–17
  meconium, 119
  places where found, 39
  seeds and corn kernels in, 119
  smell of, 119
  studies about, 118
Sideshow acts, 63
Simpson, Wallis, 91
Sinatra, Frank, 89
Skin
  dead cells in household dust,
    21
  used as a bookmark, 24
Slater, Christian, 105
Smegma, 67, 121
Smith, Will, 53

Smits, Jimmy, 89
Snakes
  biting you, 126
  eating you, 125, 126
  killed by people, 126–27
  for masturbation, 16
  spitting venom, 48, 126
Snot, 128–29
Sodomy, 130–31
Sootikins, 121
Spit, 109, 132
Springer, Jerry, 13–14, 33
Stallone, Sylvester, 4
Starr Report, 130
Stern, Howard, 72, 80
Stewart, Jon, 160
Stewart, Patrick, 89
Susann, Jacqueline, 70
Sutherland, Keifer, 89
Swayze, Patrick, 14
Sweat, 123–24

T

Tails, people with, 65–66
"Tales of Terror," 96
Tampons, 109, 134–35
Taylor, Elizabeth, 83
Teeth
  brushing, with Preparation H,
    27
  rotten, 21, 79
Television
  nipples on, 80
  tasteless, 96
Testicles
  bitten by dogs, 85
  bitten by snakes, 126
  castration, 29–33
  plastic, for dogs, 11–12
  unusual, 91, 93–94
"Texas Chainsaw Massacre," 96

The 200 Most Disgusting Sites on the Internet

$5.95, ISBN 1–58008–137–1
80 pages, 4 x 6

All real—all free. Spend hundreds of hours exploring the most disgusting (and often funniest) sites on the Internet.

You'll find hilarious **dirty songs, disgusting cartoons, outrageous graphics, tasteless postings, fabulous link sites, naughty limericks, gross new jokes,** and much, much more.

On these sites you will discover all you ever wanted to know about:

Sex & Fetishes ۞ **The Butt & the Bathroom** ۞ **The Body Disgusting** ۞ **Foul Films** ۞ **Farting Fun** ۞ **Toilet Treats** ۞ **Death and Diseases** ۞ **Sexual Records** ۞ **Horror Movies** ۞ **Odd Sex** ۞ **Boogers & Body Parts** ۞ **Crime & Cannibals** ۞ **Perverse Performers** ۞ **Weird Women** ۞ **Naughty Newsgroups** ۞ **Bizarre Magazine** ۞ **World Sexual Records** ۞ **Animal Crushing** ۞ **Barforama** ۞ **Kitty Litter Cake** ۞ **Club Mud** ۞ **The Taste Below the Waist** ۞ **Museum of Menstruation** ۞ **Insects as Food** ۞ **Masturbation** ۞ **Penis Power** ۞ **Butt Squishes** ۞ **Anal Fistulas** ۞ **Foreign Bodies Up the Ass** ۞ **Vomit Vinaigrette** ۞ **Best Curses** ۞ **Two-headed Women** ۞ **and more.**

Available from your local bookstore, or by ordering direct from the publisher. Write for our catalogs of over 1,000 books, posters, and tapes.

TEN SPEED PRESS / CELESTIAL ARTS / TRICYCLE PRESS
PO Box 7123, Berkeley, California 94707
Order phone (800) 841–2665 / Fax (510) 559–1629
Order@tenspeed.com
www.tenspeed.com